T0302520

Managing the Expansion of **Graduate Education** in Texas

Rita Karam
Charles A. Goldman
Daniel Basco
Diana Gehlhaus Carew

For more information on this publication, visit www.rand.org/t/RR1899

Library of Congress Cataloging-in-Publication Data is available for this publication.
ISBN: 978-0-8330-9744-6

Published by the RAND Corporation, Santa Monica, Calif.

Cover: Design by Next Chapter Communications/Miguel Llonch/Stocksy.

Preface

The Texas Higher Education Coordinating Board (THECB) recently adopted a new statewide strategic plan for higher education, the *60x30TX* plan. The plan calls for at least 60 percent of 25- to 34-year-olds in Texas to hold a higher education degree or certificate by 2030. Meeting this target will require significant expansion of higher education in Texas. While the plan does not set targets specifically for graduate education, the state recognizes the important role graduate education plays in advancing Texas's economic competitiveness by preparing a skilled workforce and spurring innovation.

To examine issues related to graduate education in Texas, the College for All Texans Foundation, which works to further the objectives of THECB, asked RAND Education, a unit of the RAND Corporation, to conduct this study. One goal of this study was to help THECB, higher education systems, and individual higher education institutions in Texas assess the need to expand their master's, doctoral, and professional programs. In addition, THECB expects to develop a strategic plan to align graduate education in the state with the goals of the *60x30TX* strategic plan. Findings from this study may be useful in framing issues that THECB should address in that strategic plan.

This research has been conducted by RAND Education, a unit of the RAND Corporation that conducts research on prekindergarten, K–12, and higher education issues, such as preschool quality rating systems, assessment and accountability, teacher and leader effectiveness, school improvement, out-of-school time, educational technology, and higher education cost and completion.

We circulated a draft of this report for public comment and peer review and have addressed the comments we received in this final report.

Contents

Figures

Tables

RAND CORPORATION

Managing the Expansion of **Graduate Education** in Texas

Rita Karam
Charles A. Goldman
Daniel Basco
Diana Gehlhaus Carew

Prepared for the
Texas Higher Education
Coordinating Board

EXECUTIVE SUMMARY

Graduate education is a crucial factor in meeting national, state, and local workforce needs, and in Texas the number of master's, doctoral, and professional degrees has been growing—increasing by 40 percent over the past ten years. In 2014, Texas institutions awarded about 44,000 of these degrees.

The Texas Higher Education Coordinating Board's (THECB) adoption of the 2015 *60x30TX* strategic plan is also likely to affect the number of graduate degrees. The strategic plan calls for at least 60 percent of Texans ages 25–34 to hold a quality higher education certificate or degree by 2030 (THECB, 2015a), which will require higher education institutions in Texas to increase their annual degree and certificate awards by about 80 percent over a 15-year period. Growth in annual degrees is also likely to lead to an increase in graduate education that at a minimum matches its growth rate over the past decade. Graduate education expansion needs to be well managed and directed toward the fields that need advanced skills the most; otherwise graduate programs could become misaligned with state needs and resources.

Both public institutions and private colleges offer higher education in Texas. However, Texas's higher education relies much more heavily on its public institutions to produce graduates compared to some states such as California, Florida, and New York. Texas also has an unusually complex ecosystem of public higher education compared to many states. The higher education system includes 48 public universities, of which 38 are general academic and 10 are health-related institutions. These institutions offer undergraduate programs and master's, doctoral, and professional degrees. Almost all of the universities belong to one of six different state university systems; only four institutions are not part of a system.

THECB, a state agency that oversees all public postsecondary education in Texas, is tasked with reviewing new degree programs. Programs that require more than $2 million in new investment during the first five years, as well as all new engineering degree and doctoral program proposals, require an in-depth review. Other programs can be approved without an in-depth review.

Study Goals and Objectives

While the *60x30TX* plan calls for a general expansion of higher education in Texas, this study looks at evidence from labor market data, comparisons with other states, and discussions with institution and system leaders to assess Texas's need to expand graduate degree production in particular. THECB expects to develop a strategic plan to align graduate education in the state with the goals of the *60x30TX* plan. Findings from this study may be useful in framing issues that THECB should address in that strategic plan.

Specifically this study had three objectives:

1. Assess the need to expand graduate programs in Texas public higher education institutions.
2. Provide guidance to THECB and higher education institutions on how to prepare and evaluate graduate program proposals.
3. Recommend policies to manage any needed expansion of graduate programs in Texas.

Stephen Coburn/Fotolia

Approach

We chose a mixed-method approach for this project. We used quantitative methods to assess (1) Texas's position in graduate education and research, and (2) Texas's labor market demand and need for graduate education. In addition, we conducted in-depth qualitative case studies at 12 Texas public institutions to understand what motivates institutions to expand graduate programs. In our analyses, we compared Texas to the three other largest states in the country: California, New York, and Florida. Each of these states has a significant number of universities with graduate education and research missions.

To guide the examination of the factors that influence graduate education, we first created a logic model depicted in Figure S.1 on the next page. The logic model shows the inputs, outputs, outcomes, and impacts of graduate education. While the logic model presents the factors sequentially, the reality is more complex. However, the logic model highlights critical factors for which information is available to examine the relationship from initial inputs into higher education institutions to the ultimate impacts of interest.

In this study, we focus on state competitiveness as the ultimate impact of interest for THECB and state policymakers. Inputs for public higher education institutions include research and development (R&D) obligations, state appropriations, and student tuition, which lead to high-quality research and well-prepared graduates. These outcomes help create a strong workforce, fuel innovation, promote business growth, and improve institutional prestige, ultimately strengthening the state's overall competitiveness. Students who earn graduate degrees are also likely to benefit from expanded career opportunities and higher incomes.

Figure S.1. *Logic Model*

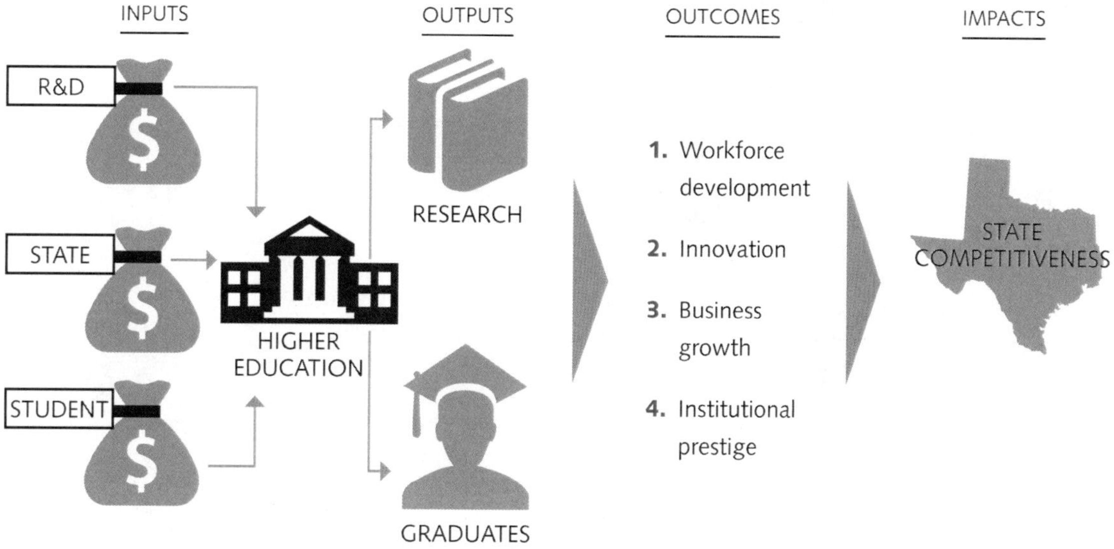

Labor Market Demand for Graduate Degrees

Labor market demand provides a critical signal about the level of education and type of skills employers are looking for, which informs the type of education universities should provide. But it is challenging for higher education institutions to measure and interpret labor market demand. They have difficulty because some graduate degrees, like undergraduate degrees, are a close match for particular occupations and others are much more generally applicable.

In this study, we examined labor market demand by estimating which occupations in Texas will likely see the largest increase in new jobs requiring a graduate degree over the next few years. Figure S.2 summarizes our projections. Across the top occupations for graduate demand, we estimate more than 120,000 new jobs requiring graduate education will be created in Texas between 2012 and 2022. As the chart shows, business, healthcare, and teachers are the groups with greatest demand.

The Texas Workforce Commission (TWC) data that we used to estimate labor market projections are based on economic forecasts and historical trends in employment. Thus projections for lawyers and perhaps other occupations may not reflect trends that have changed in these occupations since the forecasts were made.

Figure S.2. *Occupational Groups with Highest Projected Graduate Demand in Texas, 2012–22*

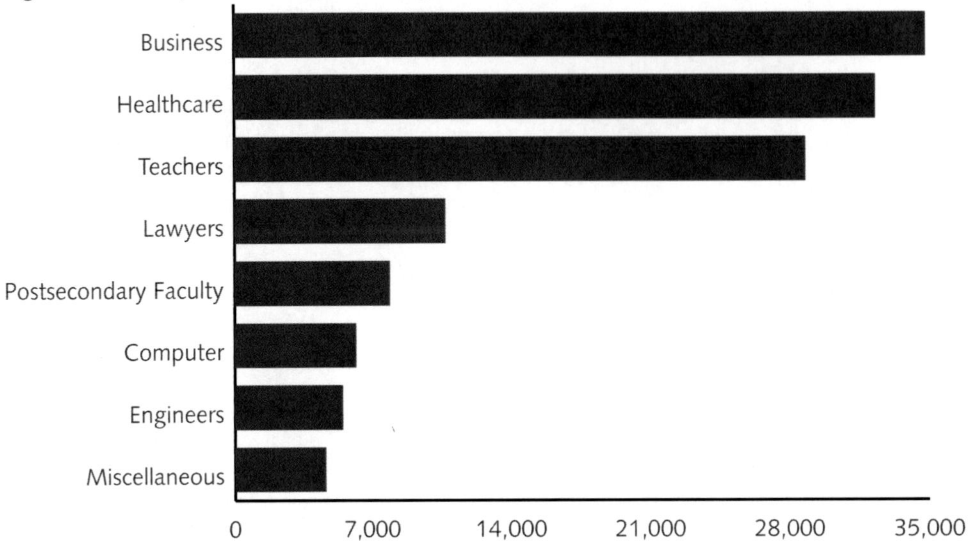

Note: Bars indicate the projected number of new jobs requiring a graduate degree created over the ten years between 2012 and 2022.

SOURCE: RAND calculations from TWC and ACS data.

Growth of Texas Degree Production

We also examined graduate degree production by broad field to understand if Texas's recent growth in graduate degree production signals a potential for the state to match future demand. Figure S.3 indicates the number of graduate degrees for Texas in 2005 and 2014 for broad fields. These fields do not map directly to the labor market data in Figure S.2 but in some cases can be compared directly to the occupational groups shown in that figure.

The chart in Figure S.3 highlights that Texas's increased graduate degree production since 2005 has mainly been in business and health fields. Graduate degree production in business fields grew by about 48 percent and in health fields by about 75 percent. The strong projected demand shown for the related occupational groups in Figure S.2 may indicate a continued need for growth in business and health graduate degrees.

Given the projected increase in graduate demand, Texas appears to be better positioned than the comparison states to produce enough graduates in education. The situation is different in engineering, however. Over the ten-year period we examined, growth in graduate engineering degrees in New York (67 percent), Florida (62 percent), and California (40 percent) outpaced growth in Texas (21 percent). But even as engineering degree production in Texas has been slow to grow, engineering jobs in the state have increased an estimated 30 percent in ten years and are projected to grow two to three times as fast as these other three states, potentially leading to unmet demand. Of course, the high production in other states may allow employers to recruit engineers from these states to meet some of their demand.

Figure S.3. *Graduate Degree Completions by Broad Field, 2005 and 2014*

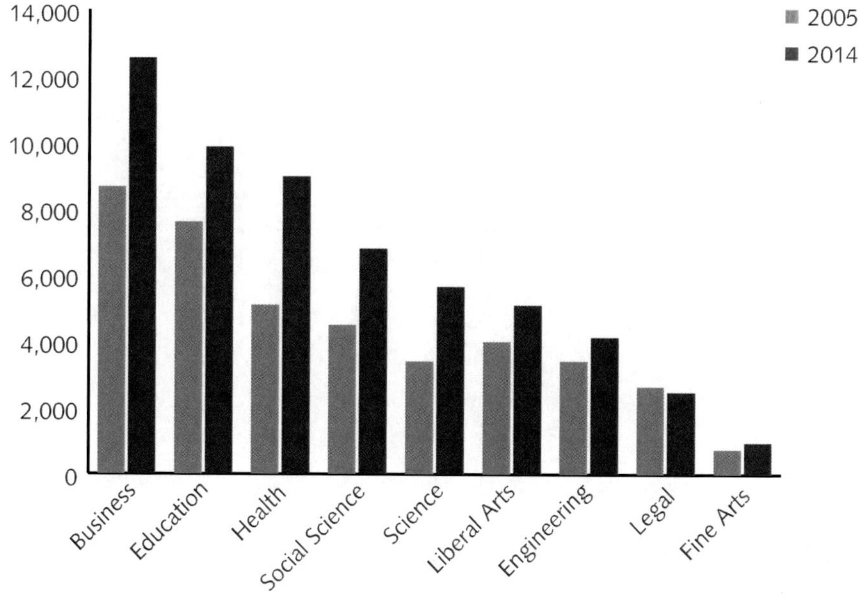

SOURCE: RAND calculations from IPEDS data.

Racial/Ethnic Composition of Graduate Degree Recipients

Texas has a large, diverse population, and its Hispanic population is growing particularly rapidly. However, Figure S.4 shows that Texas's graduate degree production does not fully reflect this reality. When looking at the racial/ethnic distribution of 2014 public institution graduate degree recipients (as a fraction of those who are citizens or permanent residents) compared to the general Texas population of 18- to 64-year-olds that year, whites and Asian-Americans are overrepresented, and Hispanics are significantly underrepresented. Public higher education institutions seeking to increase the representation of minorities in graduate education face a significant challenge, especially as Texas's population continues to grow and become more diverse.

Figure S.4. *Percentage Race/Ethnicity Distribution of Public University Graduate Degree Recipients and General Population (18- to 64-Years-Old) in Texas, 2014*

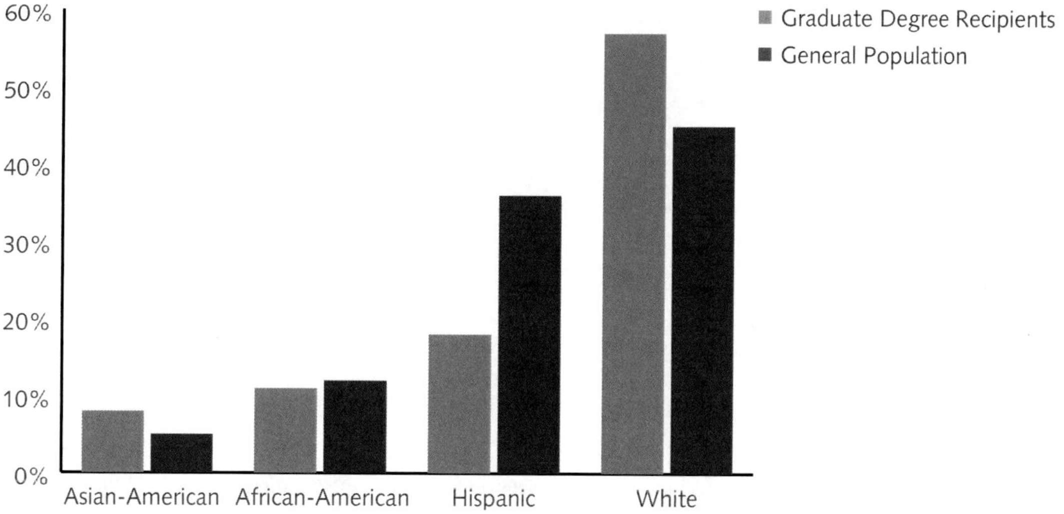

Note: Smaller racial groups omitted.

SOURCE: IPEDS and Current Population Survey.

Texas's Position in Graduate Education and Research

To this point, we have focused on historical trends to estimate how Texas's higher education ecosystem might meet a relatively straightforward concept of labor market demand, but other factors also play a key role in bolstering Texas's competitiveness and ability to attract employers. Employers who are making location decisions, especially in innovative industries that demand a base of R&D, consider a number of issues, including the broader and longer-term outcomes highlighted in the logic model in Figure S.1: workforce development, research performance, and institutional prestige. To understand Texas's standing in these areas relative to other large states, we compared Texas to California, Florida, and New York.

Graduate Degree Production

Texas has grown its graduate degree production by more than 41 percent over the ten-year period from 2005 to 2014. This increase represents the largest percentage growth of any of the states analyzed. However, Texas still remains behind California and New York in total graduate degree production. When controlling for population size, Texas's production is comparable to California's production, above Florida's, and below New York's. Unlike the comparison states, the vast majority of Texas's graduate degree production is supplied by public institutions.

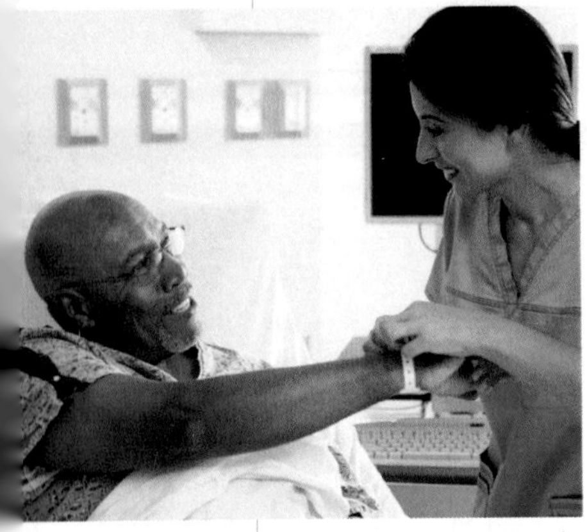

Monkey Business/Fotolia

Graduate Attainment

We also examined the overall graduate attainment rates for each state's population of 25- to 64-year-olds to understand how degree production is influencing the overall workforce. While Texas's graduate attainment is growing, it remains behind comparison states.

Research

We examined the overall funding the federal government—the top funder of research to universities—has obligated to universities from 2004 to 2013 (latest data available) to better understand how Texas has performed in this area. Despite relatively stable overall funding, Texas's share of obligations has declined in recent years. In 2013, Texas received only 34 percent of the total level of funding provided to California. Adjusting for population differences, Texas reached about 49 percent of California's funding level, 44 percent of New York's, and 156 percent of Florida's.

Ranking

Institutions that admit the brightest students and produce the greatest research also are regarded as having prestige. Graduate degree production and research funding are good signals of institutional prestige, but at the state level, another way to directly measure prestige is the number of universities recognized by the Carnegie Classification of Institutions of Higher Education, which categorizes universities by research intensity. Texas is increasing its number of Carnegie-recognized research universities faster than the others states we analyzed.

Global competition, however, is increasing, as reflected in international ranking lists. On ShanghaiRanking's global top 500 list, Texas and Florida each lost one institution between 2005 and 2015, while California and New York maintained their numbers. Looking specifically at the most competitive range, only four of the ten Texas universities in the top 500 in 2015 were ranked in the top 100. By contrast, 11 of California's 13 ranked universities were in the top 100. New York had four in the top 100, and Florida had one. This result indicates that while Texas is broadly competitive internationally, competition is increasing, and Texas has less representation at the most-competitive levels compared to California.

Strategies for Raising Competitiveness

Texas's position compared to other states and countries is important to its state competitiveness. The ranking indicators we presented in the previous section show that Texas is increasing its number of Carnegie-recognized research universities at a fast rate but, especially compared to California, is not represented at the highest levels of international competition and does not attract the same share of federal research funding. If Texas desires to further increase the competitiveness of its universities, it will likely need additional investments in research capacity.

Research universities benefit from a concentration of resources and deliberate strategies to invest in research activity (see Brewer, Gates, and Goldman, 2002; Salmi, 2009). Since California separates public universities into two systems based on mission, it can direct higher levels of funding to the research-intensive University of California campuses compared to the California State University campuses. Texas, on the other hand, allocates funding for education based on semester credit hours, broad field, and level of education but with no higher funding rates based on the research mission of certain campuses. Instead, Texas provides some state funding specifically based on research activity, recognizing that public universities need investments in research programs to promote excellence.

We found that the basic design of these funding programs is sound in aiming to increase the research capacity of Texas public institutions. The programs generally concentrate additional state resources on institutions that have already developed a measure of success in building research programs. Furthermore, they allocate funding based on measured performance in attracting research funding or, in the case of the Governor's University Research Initiative (GURI), to campuses that can attract world-class researchers from out of state.

Recommendations

To enhance the competitiveness of Texas public higher education institutions, continue, and consider increasing, state research program funding. To continue to build the competitiveness of Texas public institutions, the state should continue its research funding programs and may wish to consider increasing funding. Such increased funding could provide a greater match rate to campuses, further accelerating the development of research infrastructure on campuses that have shown some success in building nationally competitive research programs.

To enhance institutional ability to recruit key researchers from other states, consider more flexibility in the GURI. Specifically with regard to the GURI, representatives of some emerging research universities with low endowments stated that while they might be able to attract notable out-of-state researchers who would qualify for this funding, they did not have sufficient flexible funds (like endowment income) to meet the local matching requirement with nonstate funds. The state may wish to consider a more flexible approach to matching requirements that allows a broader selection of universities the opportunity to attract these researchers to Texas.

Graduate Program Decisionmaking Process

The case studies focused on analyzing the decisionmaking process at the institution level, emphasizing factors both internal and external to the institutions. From our case study interviews, we identified a number of motivators that lead institutions to propose new graduate programs. Some motivators are concerned with institutional prestige—or how an institution is positioned (as a whole or within specific fields) relative to other institutions and how it views and understands its mission. Other motivators are closer to the departmental level because they focus more on expanding specific graduate programs as a result of student or labor market demand, increased competition among graduate programs within the field, or new requirements from professional organizations. Therefore, in Figure S.5, we classified these motivators across a continuum, representing different levels at the institution.

Figure S.5. *Institutional Motivators for New Graduate Degree Programs*

Seeking Research-Intensive Status or Concentrating in a Specific Field

Texas may wish to increase the number of public research universities that are nationally and internationally competitive. However, there are challenges associated with institutional movement. One challenge is that such movement might lead to changes in the mission of the institution and affect student access, especially since institutional ranking takes into account undergraduate admission and selectivity. Another challenge is that the pressure to become a research-intensive institution may lead to the expansion of graduate programs that are not essential in meeting student or labor market demand, such as academic Ph.D. programs. This is because to become research intensive, an institution would need to have a large number of Ph.D. programs covering multiple disciplines. Institutions might establish such programs even if there is not a clear need for them in Texas's labor market.

We provide two recommendations pertaining to institutional positioning and expanding research agendas. The first relates to proposal review, and the second addresses a broader issue related to changes in institutional mission and student access.

Recommendations

Place more emphasis on institutional support and policies in reviewing doctoral program proposals. Although THECB currently considers the institution's strategic plan in its review of doctoral program proposals, it could place more emphasis on links between proposed doctoral research programs and the availability of institutional support for research as well as institutional policies conducive to research.

If the doctoral program changes the institution's strategic plan or direction, THECB could require the institution to make changes to its strategic plan first to embody and support the proposed doctoral program. However, it is important that THECB not systematically exclude institutions from expanding into doctoral education, or expanding their doctoral offerings, provided the institutions have supportive missions, strategies, resources, and policies.

Review student access regularly and consider alternative pathways when needed. Although institutions should be able to expand their research or Ph.D. programs, they and the state should also be sensitive to how such expansion could affect student admission to undergraduate programs. The institution or its system could periodically review any changes in student access. If changes in admission occur, we recommend that the institution or system explore alternatives for how to serve students who would no longer be admitted, for instance through expanding articulation with community colleges or even expanding their own student population to ensure access to less academically prepared students. THECB could provide general guidelines on how institutions could deal with student access issues if missions change.

Engaging in Positive Margin Activities

A critical objective for expanding master's programs is to generate revenue that could be used for strengthening and supporting doctoral programs. This objective is not a concern as long as the master's programs are meeting workforce and student demand and their quality has not been compromised. Although some departments have master's program accreditation review, many do not.

Recommendations

Ensure the quality of master's programs through accreditation or an alternative process. While all graduate programs must be externally evaluated at least once every seven years, institutions may opt for a specific external review if the program is not accredited by a recognized body in the academic field. One option to ensure the quality of master's programs is for them to be accredited, if accreditation for the subject matter is offered by accrediting agencies. Another option is for institutions to implement a rigorous quality assurance process that uses independent experts to assess the quality of the programs on a set of criteria that are already established in the field. Obtaining accreditation or evidence of some review by external experts is likely to improve how employers and prospective students view the legitimacy of the program, which in turn would increase an institution's competitive edge.

Develop THECB criteria for evaluating online master's program quality. THECB could also provide guidance to institutions on how to evaluate the quality of their online master's programs. Many online programs are approved as simple changes of delivery mode from existing face-to-face programs rather than undergoing a full proposal review. The Learning Technology Advisory Committee and THECB could develop criteria for reviewing online master's programs, including those changing their delivery mode. Institutions could be involved in this process or asked to provide input regarding the criteria.

Competition

Competition can be healthy and lead to innovative and high-quality programs, but it can also have a downside. Competition may generate program duplication if similar graduate programs are vying for students within the same geographic area. To keep competing programs from closing down, institutions might change their standards to attract less academically prepared students, and the quality of the programs might be affected. Furthermore, online programs, especially in education and some of the health sciences, tend to be similar and have no geographic boundaries, resulting in both increased competition for student enrollment and duplication. However, engineering online programs often do not face the same issues since these graduate programs attract international students and the supply of international students is greater compared to domestic students.

Recommendation

Avoid program duplication by promoting collaboration rather than competition at the system level. University systems could use their periodic meetings of provosts to discuss how to best manage competition among their campuses, reduce redundancy, and encourage healthy competition and collaboration. This recommendation does not mean that there should not be similar graduate programs within the same system or across systems. As long as there is student and workforce demand and the programs are of high quality and are serving various regions in Texas, duplication is not a problem. However, in instances where the student and workforce demand are insufficient and not all institutions are equally equipped to implement high-quality research graduate programs, collaboration among institutions to provide graduate education benefits the institutions, system, and state. University systems could explore ways to incentivize collaboration. They also could provide resources and technical assistance to help institutions develop joint graduate programs that emphasize institutional strengths and build on their capacities.

Labor Market Demand

Reliable employment forecasting is very challenging. Demand for new skills depends on a number of factors, including technological progress, government policies, and global conditions. For some disciplines, such as humanities, assessing demand is even more difficult because there is no clear link to one occupation, but such disciplines could be preparing students in general skills that apply to many occupations.

However, institutions could improve their mechanisms for matching their graduate programs with workforce needs by engaging in ongoing research activities and surveying employers and graduates to assess demand for skills and the quality of graduates.

Recommendations

Support institutional access to labor market analysis tools. THECB currently encourages institutions to use national and state data to determine workforce needs when proposing new graduate programs. THECB could acquire licenses or facilitate joint licenses for commercial products that simplify the use of these government data and add real-time analysis of job postings.

Provide guidance on acceptable data sources beyond the Bureau of Labor Statistics (BLS) and TWC. THECB currently encourages institutions to use BLS and TWC data to determine workforce needs when proposing new graduate programs. But such databases have shortcomings because the datasets do not map specific degrees to workforce data.

To capture labor market needs, institutions should follow traditional methods for data collection and analysis, including primary and secondary quantitative and qualitative data. THECB could support institutions by identifying some of the acceptable approaches for continually obtaining data from employers and increase institutional engagement with industry.

Provide education and training to ensure that data and tools are used wisely and effectively. THECB could help build institutions' capacity to identify workforce needs by providing training and workshops on how to use available workforce datasets, how to solicit pertinent workforce information, and how to interpret the resulting data.

Track graduate job placement. Finally, THECB could require institutions to track student job placements during the program review to see if the graduate programs have placed students in the labor market as intended. This requirement will signify to institutions the expectation to track this information and to invest in efforts to analyze labor market data more systematically. Institutions are likely to need additional resources to be able to track graduate student placement, especially at the master's level. The state could explore options for providing resources to the institutions.

Student Demand

Appropriately using student demand information to inform the expansion of programs is challenging for institutions when there is no agreed-upon measurement metric.

Recommendations

Identify best practices for measuring student demand. THECB could identify best practices and provide institutions guidelines on how to measure student demand.

Provide guidance on balancing student and labor market demands. THECB could also clarify for institutions how to balance the needs measured by student demand and labor market demand, especially in instances when such needs are misaligned.

Emerging Multidisciplinary Fields

Certain fields need graduates with multidisciplinary skills, but whether the best way to develop those skills is through a master's degree or certification is likely to vary by field and proposed program.

Recommendation

Require institutions to demonstrate a need for multidisciplinary programs. When institutions propose new multidisciplinary programs, THECB could require them to conduct more rigorous analyses of labor market needs than they would normally do. THECB could set standards by requiring institutions to articulate the benefits of the multidisciplinary program in terms of the breadth and depth of the program, the skills it promotes, and why the need being met by the proposed multidisciplinary program cannot be satisfied by restructuring existing programs in the main field through the addition of new courses or certificates.

Professional Degree Upgrading

Graduate programs in nursing, physical therapy, and other fields propose new graduate degrees to respond to professional associations. These associations advocate for advanced, often doctoral, degree programs as entry to practice, usually to support and justify a greater level of professional responsibility for practitioners. The departments that we interviewed emphasized that their responsibility is to meet employer demand and make sure their graduate students are well placed; therefore, they see a need for such programs.

Recommendation

Consider professional association standards when they are likely to shape employer demand. When evaluating new graduate programs, THECB should take into account changes in professional association standards, where they exist, to the extent they are likely to shape student and employer demand.

Systemic and Process Aspects of Graduate Program Development

In this section, we examine the pipeline of students entering science and engineering graduate programs, the state funding approach for graduate programs, the proposal development process, and ongoing program review processes.

Strengthening the Pipeline of Domestic Students into Science and Engineering Graduate Programs

While major structural factors contribute to the low enrollment of domestic students in science and engineering graduate programs, institutions, systems, and the state could all adopt programs to strengthen this pipeline and increase the representation of domestic students in Texas graduate programs. Because minority groups, especially Hispanics, are underrepresented in Texas graduate degree awards, efforts to attract more domestic students should also aim to increase the number of underrepresented students entering these graduate programs.

Recommendations

Institutions and systems should consider programs to strengthen the pipeline of domestic students, including underrepresented minorities, into science and engineering graduate programs. We think institutions and systems have opportunities to collaborate to strengthen the exposure of domestic students, including underrepresented minorities, to graduate study in science and engineering. Institutions could formally collaborate by developing pipelines through articulation agreements to transition students from undergraduate to graduate degrees.

THECB should examine plans for student stipends in new research graduate programs. Stipends are important for supporting students, especially domestic students, in research graduate programs. THECB should continue to examine proposed stipend levels and plans to fund them to ensure that stipends are adequate and competitive with other quality research graduate programs.

The state (or other funders) should consider funding special stipends for domestic students in science and engineering doctoral programs. The state, or perhaps other funders like foundations, could provide special stipends for domestic students beyond what the institutions or departments could provide. Since domestic students have options to pursue a master's degree during their career, we suggest that any special stipends be targeted specifically to domestic students in doctoral science and engineering programs (either concurrent with a master's program or following one). A portion of state research funding could be devoted to funding these additional stipends to make doctoral study more attractive.

Funding

Stakeholders have little interest in fundamental changes to the formula funding methodology, although the state should consider increases to fund the ambitious student growth goals of the *60x30TX* plan.

Recommendation

Consider increases in general fund appropriations to support growing enrollments and use the current formula funding method to allocate them. To meet the ambitious *60x30TX* goals of increased student enrollment and completions, institutions will require resources. If the state provides increased general fund appropriations that keep pace with student enrollment growth, these increases will reduce the chance that students will become burdened with escalating fees. Whatever the level of general fund appropriations, we recommend that THECB continue to use the current formula funding methodology to allocate them, although it may be prudent to monitor whether highly scalable online master's programs are attracting an increasing share of formula funding over time and, if so, consider adjustments to the formula.

Proposal Development and Review Process

The proposal process could be improved through several strategies, focusing on providing earlier, informal reviews and sharing the practices that result in successful proposals.

Recommendations

Institutions should conduct their own preproposal reviews. Since proposal development takes significant time, institutions should conduct internal preproposal reviews to direct proposal development efforts in the most productive directions.

Institutions should consult informally with THECB staff early during proposal development. Similarly, institutions should seek early, informal consultation with THECB staff to understand the experiences of other similar proposal efforts and receive guidance on which aspects of a proposal are likely to receive the greatest scrutiny.

Provide guidance on the characteristics of successful proposals. To generalize and extend the consultation function, THECB could compile guidance on the aspects associated with the most successful proposals. This guidance could help institutions and departments as they prepare future proposals.

Ongoing Program Review Processes

THECB generally has limited powers to review programs after they have been approved, with two major exceptions: periodic doctoral program reviews and low-producing programs. Doctoral programs are required to report to THECB annually for five years and then at least every seven years after that. Under the recent revisions to its mandate, THECB no longer has the authority to order the closure of degree programs with low enrollment or production. Instead, the state now relies on an annual report from THECB on low-producing programs that identifies degree programs at each institution that have been operating at least five years and where the number of graduates has fallen below a specified threshold over a five-year period (25 for undergraduate, 15 for master's, and 10 for doctoral).

Recommendation

Continue policies and practices for program review and low-producing programs; review consolidation proposals closely. The doctoral program review and low-producing programs report seem to be helpful in managing graduate programs. One area we recommend for further scrutiny is proposed consolidations of graduate programs. Further scrutiny could prevent the funding of consolidations that do not entail meaningful integration of the academic programs.

Conclusion

Texas's higher education ecosystem is large and complex. Because Texas depends very heavily on its public universities to train graduates, produce research, and spur innovation, policies that affect the public university sector are even more important for maintaining and enhancing competitiveness in Texas than in other states that benefit from prestigious private universities.

Texas's *60x30TX* strategic plan and our analysis of labor market projections point to a continuation of the past 10 years of strong growth in graduate education in the state. Generally, Texas has been increasing its production of graduate degrees in fields corresponding to the occupational groups that are expected to have the most job openings: business, healthcare, education, computers, and engineering. However, because growth in graduate engineering degrees has been slow compared to other states and to projected demand, THECB and institutions should consider expanding graduate programs in engineering. In addition, THECB and institutions should expand efforts to recruit domestic students and provide adequate financial support to motivate those with a bachelor's degree to pursue graduate education.

George Wada/Fotolia

To be competitive, Texas needs to compare favorably to other states and countries. The number of research universities in Texas is increasing rapidly compared to other states, but too few of these institutions are ranked at the highest levels internationally. Texas's institutions also do not attract the same share of federal R&D funding as other states, especially California. To further increase the competitiveness of its universities, Texas will likely need to make additional public investments in research capacity for institutions at several stages of development. However, these investments must be focused on institutions that have shown at least some capability to develop research programs.

As Texas explores ways to increase graduate education production, it can look at increasing enrollments in existing programs, but new programs will likely be necessary as well. Developing new programs presents the state and institutions both opportunities and challenges. Proposals for new programs must be evaluated carefully to ensure that they maximize the benefits to Texas and the United States. While expanding graduate programs and research is an opportunity to build institutional prestige, it can also be unproductive if institutions expand in areas not related to state economic needs. Institutions may also seek to develop large-scale online programs to increase operating margins in the face of constrained state funding. These programs may expand access and increase revenue, but they may also dilute quality.

If an institution seeks to shift to a research-intensive mission, it must make a widespread, sustained commitment, starting with developing a thoughtful strategic plan and then aligning its graduate program proposals with that strategic plan. Other universities may choose to focus on specific niches by proposing graduate degree programs that match their specific capabilities or context and that may not be available at other institutions.

Expanding graduate programs is important for meeting the goals of THECB's *60x30TX* plan and for improving Texas's state competitiveness. However, this expansion must be managed well to ensure that the programs are high quality. While institutions are responsible for monitoring the quality of their graduate programs, THECB and accrediting agencies can support quality through their program approval and review processes. The recommendations presented in this report are intended as guidance for THECB on how to strengthen its current review and approval process and how to help institutions determine whether there is a need to expand their graduate education programs. Some of the recommendations also provide guidance for institutions and systems on how to manage competition and promote quality in graduate programs.

Monkey Business/Fotolia

Acknowledgments

The authors would like to thank the commissioner, staff, and board members of THECB for helpful guidance throughout the research process, with particular acknowledgment to Rex Peebles, Stacey Silverman, Allen Michie, James Goeman, Paul Turcotte, David Gardner, Julie Eklund, and Nina Wright.

We appreciate the members of the Graduate Education Advisory Committee interacting with us at several stages of the study, sharing their insights and feedback on drafts of our work. We also thank the participants in our interviews. Although we agreed not to name them or their institutions, we deeply appreciate their cooperation and the important information they shared with our research team. We appreciate the universities and systems that provided us comments on the draft report, which helped us improve this final version.

We thank RAND colleagues Chandra Garber and Erin-Elizabeth Johnson for helping us communicate our findings in a clear and engaging way. We greatly appreciate the thoughtful input of our external reviewer, Jonathan Gagliardi, and internal reviewers, Catherine Augustine and Susan Gates, on the drafts of this report and study briefings. We also thank Next Chapter Communications for designing and laying out this report.

1 Introduction

Many studies document the need for graduate education and its advantages. First, for the United States to stay competitive in the global economy, its higher education institutions need to be able to produce sufficient numbers of graduate degree holders who are trained to think critically, be innovative, and develop solutions to challenges facing the United States and other countries. Second, demand in the U.S. labor market has increased for advanced degrees, and graduate education plays an important role in meeting that demand. A 2012 report by the Council of Graduate Schools and Educational Testing Service estimated that approximately 2.6 million new and replacement jobs would require a graduate degree. It also projected that by 2020 "the number of jobs requiring a master's degree will increase by about 22%, while the number of jobs requiring a doctorate or professional degree is expected to increase by 20%." These projections indicate a shift in the labor market, where opportunities for those with advanced skills and knowledge are growing.

Graduate degrees are strongly associated with higher salaries for individuals. Both male and female workers with graduate degrees earn significantly more than their less-educated counterparts. In addition, the wage premium associated with graduate education generally increases with the level of educational attainment, as shown in Figures 1.1 and 1.2. The figures show a clear increase in wages for each level of postsecondary education relative to high school graduates.

Moreover, the figures show that the wage premium associated with graduate education for men and women is generally widening over time, as real earnings for high school graduates have stagnated. For example, in 1991, real average annual earnings of men working full time with a doctoral degree were about $110,000, compared to $46,000 for men with a high school diploma (in 2015 dollars). By 2015, these numbers were $143,000 and $48,000 respectively, a difference almost twice as large as in 1991. In other words, by 2015, male workers with doctoral degrees earned almost three times as much as male high school graduates on average. Similarly, although slightly less stark than for men, the real average annual earnings premium for women working full time with a doctoral degree was almost $45,000 more than for women with a high school diploma in 1991, rising to $68,000 by 2015 (in 2015 dollars). For master's and professional degrees the earnings premium compared to high school diploma increased between 33 and 55 percent over this period.

Figure 1.1. *Male Real Average Annual Earnings, Full-Time Workers Ages 18 and Older, 1991–2015 (in 2015$)*

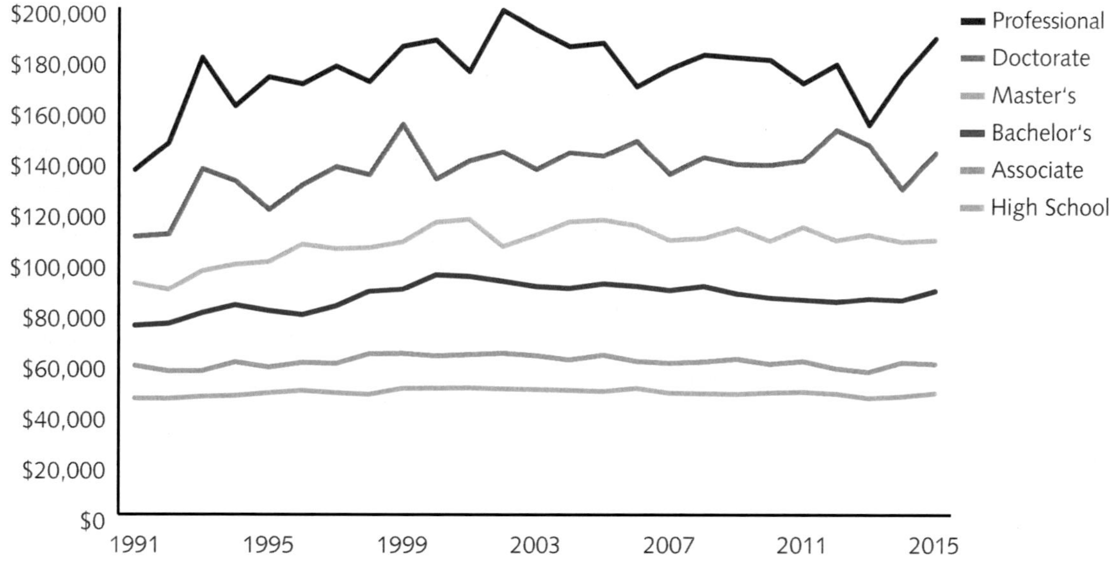

SOURCE: U.S. Census, Table P.32.

Figure 1.2. *Female Real Average Annual Earnings, Full-Time Workers Ages 18 and Older, 1991–2015 (in 2015$)*

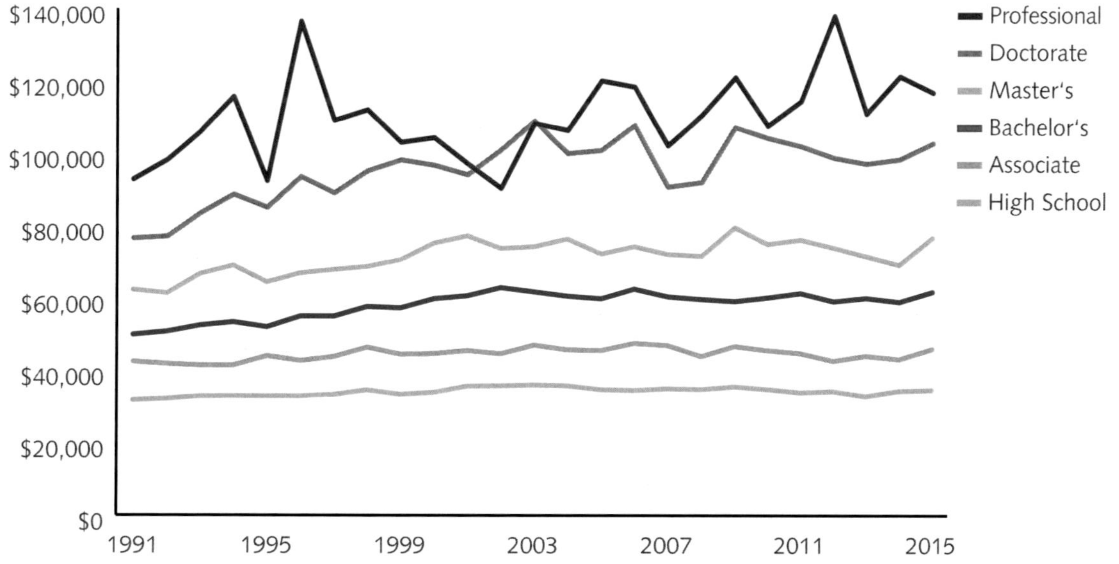

SOURCE: U.S. Census, Table P.32.

Furthermore, data from the Bureau of Labor Statistics also show that unemployment rates for master's and doctoral degree holders are much lower than for those holding a bachelor's degree or less, and these gaps in unemployment increase during economic downturns (Council of Graduate Schools and Educational Testing Service, 2012).

Graduate Education in Texas

The state of Texas recognizes the need for graduate education and its benefits in serving national, state, and local workforce needs. Graduate education in Texas has been growing, with the number of graduate awards—specifically master's, doctoral, and professional degrees—increasing by 40 percent over the past ten years. In 2014, Texas institutions awarded about 44,000 of these degrees. Furthermore, the Texas Higher Education Coordinating Board (THECB), a state agency that oversees all public postsecondary education in Texas, adopted in 2015 the new *60x30TX* strategic plan for higher education that might necessitate more graduate education expansion (THECB, 2015a). The *60x30TX* plan calls for at least 60 percent of Texans ages 25–34 to hold a quality higher education certificate or degree by 2030. To achieve this goal, higher education institutions in Texas will need to increase their annual degree and certificate awards by about 80 percent between 2015 and 2030. While the *60x30TX* plan does not set specific targets for graduate education, the general expansion of degree awards is likely to lead to graduate education growing at least as much as in the last decade, perhaps even more.

Graduate degree expansion, of course, can serve important state and local workforce needs. But there is also concern that graduate programs might be misaligned with state needs and resources if expansion is not well managed and directed toward the fields that need advanced skills the most. However, managing expansion is challenging because there is a gap in time between recognizing the occupation need and having education institutions supply graduates with skills to fill that need.

Higher education in Texas is offered primarily by public institutions but also by private colleges and universities. Compared to some other states like California and New York, Texas relies heavily on its public institutions to produce graduates. Texas also has an unusually complex ecosystem of public higher education. The state has 48 public universities, including 38 general academic and 10 health-related institutions, which offer undergraduate programs and master's, doctoral, and professional degrees. As of 2014, Texas public universities and health-related institutions offered about 2,300 graduate programs. Almost all of the universities belong to one of six different state university systems, while four institutions are not part of a system. Each system contains institutions with a wide range of missions, so THECB has developed a set of accountability peer groups to identify institutions with broadly similar missions, even if they are members of different systems or are independent. The grouping assignments are not permanent and are subject to revision as institutions evolve. The peer groups are

- research university: generates at least $150 million of restricted research expenditure and offers a comprehensive range of graduate programs including master's, professional doctoral, and Ph.D. programs

Frank/Fotolia

- emerging research university: generates at least $30 million of research expenditure and offers a wide range of master's, professional doctoral, and Ph.D. programs
- doctoral university: offers master's and professional doctoral programs and has a small number of Ph.D. programs in selected fields
- comprehensive university: offers master's programs and may offer doctoral programs in small number of fields
- master's university: offers master's programs
- health related: is not classified into a specific peer group.

The distribution of institutions by peer group is presented in Table 1.1 below.

Table 1.1. *Distribution of Public Universities by Peer Group, 2015*

Peer Group	Institutions
Research	2
Emerging Research	8
Doctoral	7
Comprehensive	6
Master's	15
Health Related	10
Total	**48**

Graduate Program Development and Review Process

THECB is tasked with reviewing new degree programs. Programs that require more than $2 million in new investment during the first five years, as well as all new engineering degree and doctoral program proposals, require an in-depth review. Other programs can be approved without an in-depth review. THECB has developed criteria to which institutions are required to respond when proposing a new graduate program. Both the proposed master's and doctoral programs are expected to provide evidence on

- labor market and student demand
- student recruitment and enrollment projections
- relevancy of courses and appropriateness of credit hours
- accreditation
- availability of qualified faculty
- availability of a library and facilities
- projected program costs and revenues
- plans to monitor and evaluate the quality of the program.

However, THECB requires institutions to provide more rigorous and detailed evidence for proposed doctoral programs than for master's programs. In addition, THECB requires institutions from selected peer groups to provide a copy of their strategic plans when they propose doctoral programs to explain how the programs will build on and expand the institution's existing recognized strengths. THECB also requires institutions to provide information on the research capacity of faculty and availability of research support for students for their proposed doctoral programs.

In regards to proposed online doctoral programs, institutions are requested to provide evidence regarding the quality of the online aspect of instruction. The Learning Technology Advisory Committee (LTAC) reviews and makes recommendations to THECB regarding proposed online doctoral programs to ensure the development of high-quality programs. Proposed online master's programs are required to meet only the criteria that apply to face-to-face programs and do not undergo this additional review.

Study Goals and Objectives

The state of Texas and its institutions have an ongoing interest in graduate education, including master's, doctoral, and professional programs. But the state, as well as its major systems of higher education, must manage various forces to align proposed graduate programs with the needs and resources of the state.

While the *60x30TX* plan calls for a general expansion of higher education in Texas, this study looks at evidence from labor market data, comparisons with other states, and discussions with institution and system leaders to assess Texas's need to expand graduate degree production in particular. THECB expects to develop a strategic plan to align graduate education in the state with the goals of the *60x30TX* plan. Findings from this study may be useful in framing issues that THECB should address in that strategic plan.

Specifically this study had three objectives:

1. Assess the need to expand graduate programs in Texas public higher education institutions.
2. Provide guidance to THECB and higher education institutions on how to prepare and evaluate graduate program proposals.
3. Recommend policies to manage any needed expansion of graduate programs in Texas.

Organization of This Report

This report continues with Chapter 2, which explains the tasks, methods, and data sources for assessing the need to expand graduate programs in Texas higher education institutions. Chapter 3 discusses the extent to which the Texas graduate education ecosystem's degree production is aligned with projected workforce demand and compares the Texas graduate education ecosystem with ecosystems in California, Florida, and New York. Chapter 4 assesses Texas's position in graduate education and research on a variety of indicators and compares it with the position in California, Florida, and New York. It also provides recommendations on how to increase Texas's competitiveness in graduate education. Chapter 5 examines factors that motivate institutions to expand their graduate programs and provides recommendations to improve the preparation and evaluation of proposed graduate programs. Chapter 6 discusses systemic and process aspects of graduate program development, including the state funding approach and program review processes, and recommends ways to enhance these approaches and processes. Chapter 7 concludes the report by summarizing the findings and discussing key recommendations.

2 Study Approach and Data Sources

In this chapter, we discuss the approach we took and the data and methods we used. We also address limitations of the study.

Approach

We chose a mixed-method approach for this project. We used quantitative methods to assess (1) Texas's position in graduate education and research, and (2) Texas's labor market demand and need for graduate education. In addition, we conducted in-depth qualitative case studies to understand what motivates institutions to expand graduate programs. The study approach included seven tasks that we describe below.

Task 1. Review Graduate Degree Program Inventory

We reviewed THECB's inventory of graduate programs and analyzed information on the number and type of proposed graduate programs that were submitted to THECB for review as well as the approval rate for the past ten years. We interviewed THECB staff about their graduate programs and current graduate degree review and approval processes and evaluation criteria. Based on this information, we developed criteria that describe the different aims and markets of the graduate programs. These criteria guided the development of instruments used in this study to obtain information on how institutions make decisions regarding program expansion and what factors motivate their decisions.

Task 2. Review Other States' Policies and Practices

We identified a sample of states—California, Florida, and New York—that have higher education ecosystems comparable to that of Texas in terms of size and breadth. We conducted interviews with state and institutional stakeholders representing higher education systems in those states and reviewed their policies to understand how they manage the distribution and potential expansion of graduate programs at their public universities. The goal of the interviews was to inform policy choices available to Texas regarding graduate program expansion.

Task 3. Assess Texas's Position in Graduate Education and Research

To assess Texas's position compared to other states, we developed a logic model (described on page 25) that links inputs, outputs, and outcomes to the impacts of graduate education on Texas's state competitiveness. We used the logic model to identify constructs and indicators that operationalize the various constructs. For each indicator we calculated scores and compared them across Texas, California, Florida, and New York to provide a context for Texas's position.

Task 4. Compare Program Offerings to State Economic Needs, Strategic Goals, and the Labor Market

In considering the benefits of expanding graduate programs in Texas, it is important to understand whether the current programs are responsive to the economic needs of the state. We analyzed the major national and Texas-specific data sources most commonly used in measuring workforce supply and demand, as well as in linking workforce needs to educational needs. We used these data first to estimate the share of workers with a graduate degree by detailed occupation. Next, we used Texas state employment projections to estimate the number of new jobs requiring a graduate degree that will be created between 2012 and 2022, using the calculated 2012 graduate share. Then, we ranked the top 40 occupations based on these estimates. Finally, we categorized these occupations into several aggregated groups. For additional context, we further calculated growth rates for the projected top occupations requiring a graduate degree across three comparison states—California, Florida, and New York. We discuss trends and implications for these occupations across the three states relative to Texas.

Task 5. Conduct Case Studies in Example Fields

We conducted case studies to understand the decisionmaking process and factors that motivate institutions to expand their graduate programs. We used purposive sampling for selecting institutions and fields, which allowed us to select institutions and fields that represent a variety of contexts. Specifically, we included 12 institutions in the case studies that represent all peer groups, since motivations might vary by institutions' research status. We also focused our examination on six fields—education, nursing, physical therapy, geographic information systems (GIS), electrical engineering, and statistics—to understand in-depth issues that influence institutions' decisions to propose new graduate programs. These fields were selected taking into consideration student demand, institutional demand, presence of emerging fields, projected job growth, lack of identified career paths, and variety in size and disciplines covered. For each field, we interviewed stakeholders from at least two different higher education institutions that currently offer graduate programs in the field and different employers of graduates to get stakeholder input about the quality of the graduate program, student characteristics, and preparation and job placement. Interviews also captured information on the current and projected workforce needs in five of the six studied fields and how higher education institutions in Texas could meet those needs.[1]

Task 6. Interview Texas University System Leaders

We interviewed leaders from three Texas university systems regarding policy options and influences that need to be taken into account when making decisions about expanding graduate programs.

Task 7. Recommend Ways to Improve Proposal Preparation and Review

We used the analysis conducted in Tasks 1 through 6 to recommend appropriate ways to use information about labor markets and other benefits of graduate programs. These recommendations are intended to strengthen existing processes for preparing, reviewing, and approving proposals. We also identified principles to guide policy decisions and recommended options that Texas can use to manage graduate program expansion. The principles are discussed in Chapters 5 and 6.

Recommendations are found in Chapters 4, 5, and 6. The study conclusion is provided in Chapter 7.

---

1 Although we made a number of contacts, we did not find employers in the field of nursing to participate in our interviews.

Data Sources and Analysis

We used a mixed-method analysis and multiple data sources to examine the need for institutions to expand graduate programs and how decisions regarding expansions are made. As noted, we relied on available secondary quantitative data to assess Texas's position in graduate education and research and to compare program offerings to state economic needs. We developed a set of indicators for Texas's position and degree production using the logic model described below. We also reviewed state policies regarding program expansion and interviewed stakeholders to understand the factors that motivate institutions to propose or expand new programs and to capture views on graduate program needs and quality.

Quantitative Data and Logic Model for Indicators

To understand the factors that influence graduate education, we created a logic model that diagrams the relationship from initial inputs into higher education institutions to the ultimate impacts of interest. Figure 2.1 below outlines the relationships among inputs, outputs, outcomes, and impacts in graduate education. The logic model presents the factors sequentially, while in reality the process is more complex. However, the logic model sheds light on critical factors on which information is available to examine the relationships among the various factors and impacts of graduate education.

Given our focus on public higher education institutions, we identified overall state competitiveness as the ultimate impact of interest for THECB and state policymakers. To improve state competitiveness, public higher education institutions use research and development (R&D) obligations, state appropriations, and student tuition to produce high-quality research and well-prepared graduates. These graduates help create a strong workforce for the state and the nation. In addition, research and human capital help fuel innovation, business growth, and institutional prestige, especially in highly populated areas (and to a much lesser extent in other local communities). These outcomes from higher education institutions ultimately strengthen the state's overall competitiveness. Of course, students who earn graduate degrees may also benefit from expanded career opportunities and higher incomes.

Figure 2.1. *Logic Model*

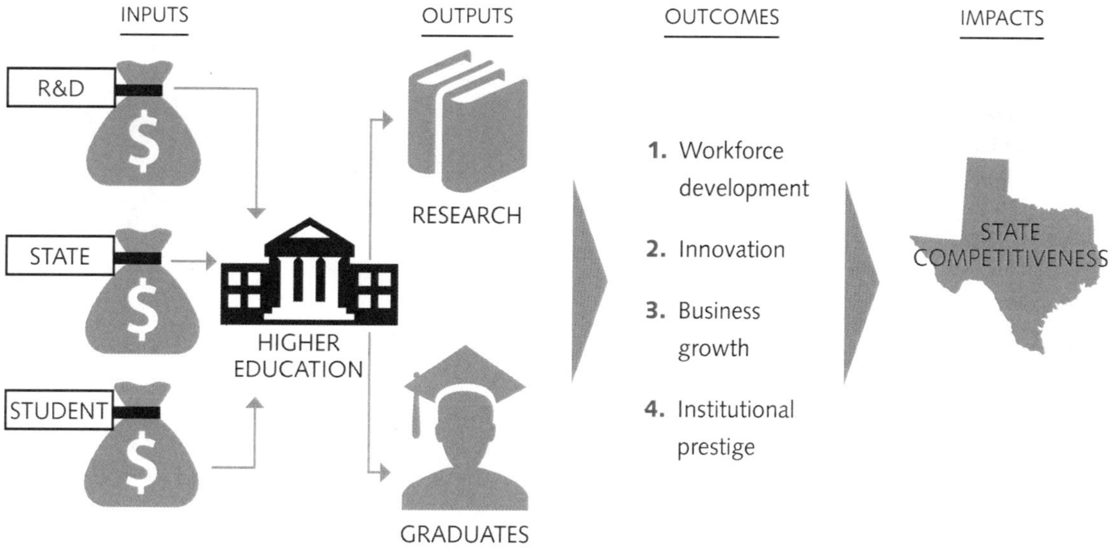

Throughout the next two chapters, we describe various aspects of the higher education ecosystem that we identified in the logic model to better understand the current state of graduate education in Texas.

Appendix Table A.1 provides detail on the data sources we used to develop indicators of the concepts depicted in the logic model.

Qualitative Data

In the section below, we describe the sampling and data collection procedures for the case studies and noncase study interviews (employer, university system, and state interviews). Case study data were collected from February through May 2015. Noncase study data were collected from May through August 2015. Table 2.1 shows the total number of interviewees by stakeholder group.

Table 2.1. *Interviews Conducted*

Organization Type	Institutions	Participants
Texas Higher Education Institutions	12	145
Texas University Systems	3	7
Other State University Systems	3	6
Employers	8	8
Total	**26**	**166**

CASE STUDIES

We used purposive sampling to select 12 Texas higher education institutions for our case studies. The institutions were selected to represent a variety of contexts, peer-group classifications, and geographic locations. We visited each institution to understand the broad range of experiences and perspectives with respect to how institutions make decisions regarding the expansion of graduate programs. Table 2.2 shows the distribution of the 12 institutions across the peer groups. Because graduate programs, particularly the most complex doctoral programs, are concentrated in the research and emerging research peer groups, we allocated a little more than half of the sample to these groups, while distributing the rest of the sample to include one each in the other general academic peer groups and two in the health-related group.

Table 2.2. *Distribution of Case Study Institutions*

Peer Group	Institutions
Research	2
Emerging Research	5
Doctoral	1
Comprehensive	1
Master's	1
Health Related	2
Total	**12**

Since visiting each department or college at each institution was not feasible, our examination focused on six fields across the 12 institutions. This focus allowed us to examine in-depth issues that influence institutions' decisions to propose new graduate programs. The six fields were education, nursing, physical therapy, engineering, GIS, electrical engineering, and statistics. To capture a wide range of perspectives, we considered several factors in selecting the fields including (1) domestic and international student demand represented by the number of the graduate awards granted by higher education institutions in each field, (2) institutional demand for specific fields represented by the number of proposals for graduate programs submitted to THECB, (3) the presence of emerging fields that are expected to grow but are currently represented by a small number of awards, (4) projected growth in jobs, (5) lack of identified career paths, and (6) variety in size and disciplines covered.

Teams of two RAND researchers spent approximately two days at each institution. During each visit, we met with institutional leaders including presidents/vice presidents, provosts/associate provosts, and deans of graduate schools. We also met with department leaders, including chairs/associate chairs, and program directors representing at least two of the six selected fields.

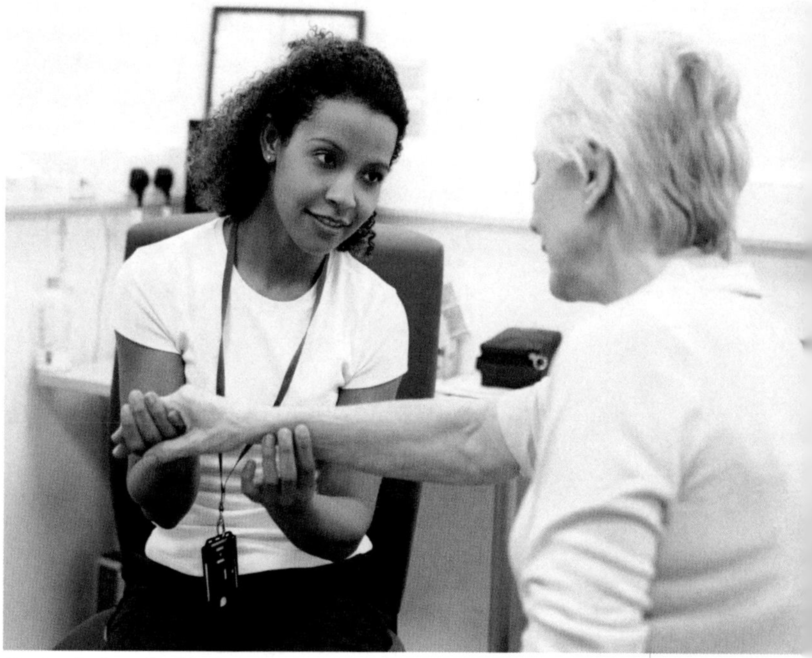

Monkey Business/Fotolia

We developed two sets of interview protocols: one for institutional leaders and the other for department leaders. The institutional leader protocol sought information about the institution's overall strategy regarding graduate program expansion. The protocol addressed topics such as (1) the institution's mission and rationale for having graduate programs, (2) overall strategies used to compete or collaborate with other institutions on graduate programs, (3) factors considered in pursuing or expanding graduate programs, (4) mechanisms for monitoring the quality of graduate programs, and (5) the role of financial support in expanding graduate programs. The department-level protocol addressed similar topics but focused on graduate programs within a specific field. The department protocol also sought information about the characteristics of students in the graduate programs, the delivery modes of degree programs, the skills developed by the programs, and student and workforce demand for such programs. For those departments that were in the process of proposing new programs or had just established one, we asked them to discuss the process and what led them to make the expansion decision.

EMPLOYER PHONE INTERVIEWS

During the case study visits, we asked department leaders to provide us with the names of employers of their graduates and to identify individuals likely to have the most knowledge about the graduate program. We made a list of employers for each of the six fields and selected a sample from each field to contact. We conducted phone interviews with hiring managers and human resources. The phone interviews elicited information about trends in the specific field and related occupations, whether Texas's workforce and higher education institutions are responsive to those trends, and whether there is a need for graduate degrees in the specific occupations. Employers were also asked about the quality of graduates and whether higher education institutions in Texas are preparing students and developing the necessary skills to meet occupational demand.

UNIVERSITY SYSTEM LEADER PHONE INTERVIEWS

We interviewed leaders of three Texas higher education systems to ask about their program approval processes, strategic planning for graduate education and research, and competition and collaboration among institutions within and outside their systems. For broader context on graduate degree approval processes, our research also included similar interviews with leaders from the California and New York state systems.

DOCUMENT REVIEW

For three states—California, Florida, and New York—we reviewed official documentation regarding the structure and organization of higher education, along with the processes and policies associated with approving new graduate degree programs.

ANALYSIS

We analyzed the case study notes and other stakeholder interviews and incorporated findings from the document review where relevant. Specifically, after each site visit and employer and state interview, RAND researchers discussed the notes and extracted main findings covering the general topics addressed in the protocols. Themes were extracted for each site, field, and type of graduate program (e.g., Ph.D., master's, etc.). RAND researchers then reviewed the main findings, tabulated them, and extracted common themes across sites using Excel software, as well as identified themes that are site, field, or graduate program specific.

Study Limitations

As with any study of this kind, we faced limitations. The case studies collected information from a sample of 12 institutions out of the 48 institutions representing the various peer groups and geographic areas. While the institutions did not appear to us to be atypical in any way from the rest of the institutions, the case study findings reflect this specific set of institutions and the six study fields. Although the case study data were self-reported we enhanced the validity of our findings by interviewing multiple staff members at each institution, both at the administrative and departmental levels. Obtaining data on quality from multiple sources is a method commonly used to obtain reliable measures of complex processes such as decisionmaking. Furthermore, the fact that common themes regarding how institutions decide to propose new programs emerged from various data sources and across sites increased our confidence in the results. Finally, we shared preliminary themes with the Graduate Education Advisory Committee, which includes graduate deans and other faculty and administrators representing 24 higher education institutions in Texas (including two private universities), to obtain their input and increase the soundness of the findings.

As we discuss in Chapter 3, the quantitative analysis of labor market demands provided a general indication of potential future demands, but since these forecasts were based on projecting historical trends, actual experience may have varied from the projections. The quantitative indicators of Texas's position relative to other states warrant some caution in interpretation since these indicators are proxies for underlying concepts illustrated in our logic model and may also be influenced by the specific context in each state.

3 Texas Labor Market Demand and Degree Production

We start this chapter by describing different motivations for pursuing graduate degrees and their links to societal value and economic production. We then consider how Texas's graduate education ecosystem is positioned to meet future labor market needs. Trained graduates represent part of the output stage of the logic model shown in Figure 2.1. In this chapter, we first consider the available projections of Texas labor market demand that may inform planning future graduate degree production. Then we examine degree production in Texas over the past ten years to understand the ways that the ecosystem may be aligned, or misaligned, with projected demand. For both labor market projections and degree production, we examine the situation in Texas with comparisons to California, Florida, and New York. We also examine the representation of racial and ethnic groups in graduate degrees awarded in Texas.

Labor Market Demand for Graduate Degrees

To better understand labor market demand, as part of this study we estimated which occupations in Texas will likely see the largest increase in new jobs requiring a graduate degree over the next few years. To do this analysis, we built upon previous RAND research that examined workforce demand in Texas more generally for degree planning. The report, *Using Workforce Information for Degree Program Planning in Texas* (Goldman et al., 2015), identified occupations that were candidates for expanded postsecondary education programs based on specified quantitative criteria, such as projected growth and educational attainment of workers in the occupation, and qualitative criteria, such as industry expert and employer interviews. This analysis extended that work by specifically identifying occupations with demand for graduate education.

As in the previous project, we used national and state employment projections over the 2012–22 time period, which are the most recent Texas projections available. This analysis considered all occupations, as classified in the Standard Occupational Classification (SOC) manual. To obtain the shares of those employed in a given occupation in Texas with graduate education, we used RAND estimates derived from the American Community Survey (ACS) for 2012 Texas residents. We next created a crosswalk to match ACS codes with SOC codes.[2]

To obtain the number of new jobs requiring a graduate education between 2012 and 2022, we applied the graduate share to the total number of estimated new jobs created for each occupation. We note that this estimate of demand is conservative because it considers only new jobs created, not turnover and job replacements. If the current education ecosystem is sized to produce sufficient graduates to fill natural

2 Though the matching was not one-to-one, we matched codes as closely as possible with some duplication.

replacements, then our estimate of new graduate jobs represents additional capacity that the education ecosystem must fill.

Next, we ranked the occupations by projected number of new jobs requiring a graduate degree between 2012 and 2022 and retained all occupations with a projected demand of 1,000 graduate degrees or more. This list included 42 occupations.

For presentation purposes, we consolidated these top 42 occupations into several occupational groups. Figure 3.1 provides the estimates by occupational category. Across the top 42 occupations, we estimate more than 120,000 new jobs requiring graduate education will be created in Texas between 2012 and 2022. As the chart shows, business, healthcare, and teachers are the groups with greatest demand. These groups include business occupations such as accountants and financial analysts, healthcare occupations such as nurses and physical therapists, and teaching occupations such as elementary and secondary school teachers. Full details on the top 42 occupations are provided in Appendix Table A.2.

Postsecondary faculty are also projected to have significant demand over this period. Indeed, if the *60x30TX* plan's ambitious goal to increase higher education awards by 80 percent over 15 years is met, the sector will require significant hiring of new faculty. The Texas Workforce Commission (TWC) data that we used for our projections are based on economic forecasts and historical trends in employment. As a result, if conditions that affect an occupation change significantly after the forecasts are made, the forecasts can become inaccurate. For instance, using historical trends, TWC projects an increase in demand of 10,700 for lawyers between 2012 and 2022, but that forecast may be inaccurate given the widespread reports of difficulties that new attorneys are having in finding work related to their degree and low demand for attorneys in general (Olson, 2015; McEntee, 2016). While we are not specifically aware of discussions that cast doubt on projections for other occupations, it is important not to rely only on these forecasts when assessing the need for new or expanded degree programs.

We also examined data on the growth of these occupations over the past several years. According to our calculations from ACS data for Texas, graduate-linked occupations in business, healthcare, teachers, postsecondary faculty, and engineers experienced growth of 21 to 27 percent over the seven years between 2006 and 2013 (the longest period available in the data).[3] These growth rates were noteworthy on their own and all the more so considering that the Great Recession depressed employment in the middle of the period. If these trends extended for a ten-year period (matching the period of TWC's projections), they would represent growth rates of 29 to 39 percent.

3 We examined 28 of the 42 top graduate occupations, where consistent data were available. Because of changes in the definitions and groupings of occupations we could not include the other 14 occupations, which included lawyers and all of the computer-related occupations.

Figure 3.1. *Occupational Groups with Highest Projected Graduate Demand in Texas, 2012–22*

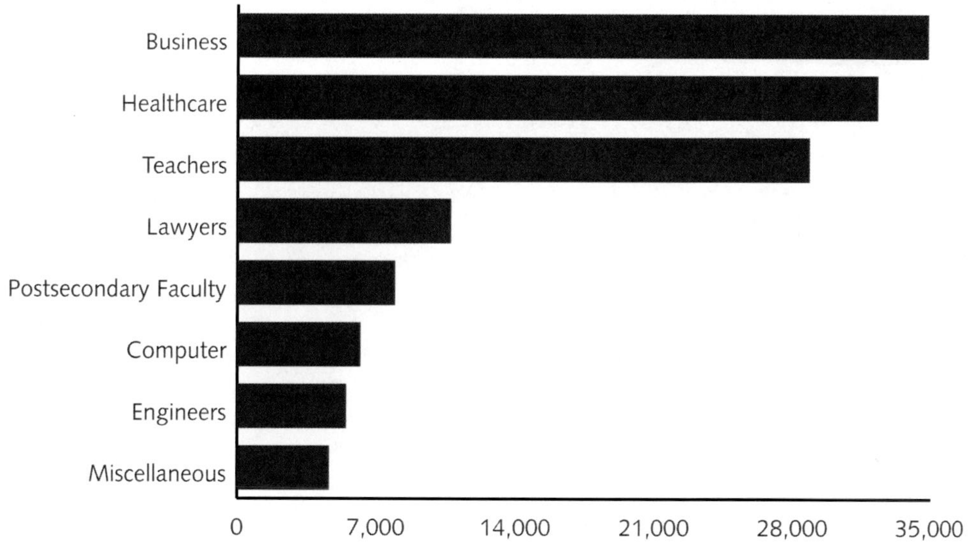

Note: Bars indicate the projected number of new jobs requiring a graduate degree created over the ten years between 2012 and 2022.

SOURCE: RAND calculations from TWC and ACS data.

We made our projections based on a constant share of workers requiring a graduate degree in each occupation. It is possible that the share of graduate education in a given occupation is increasing over time, making the number of required graduate degrees even larger. These shares could be increasing both because the skills required to complete the tasks for the occupation are increasing and simply because more people are obtaining graduate degrees. The rise in bachelor's degree recipients may well be encouraging more people to use graduate education as an enhanced labor market signal, regardless of whether or not the eventual job placements require graduate-level training. We analyzed ACS data to try to estimate the change in graduate share by occupation for our top occupations, but the estimates were much too imprecise to use for projections.

Although the ACS data do not enable reliable estimates of graduate shares over time at the occupational level, we do find evidence to suggest that graduate shares across occupations are generally increasing over time. This finding is consistent with observable trends in the rise of graduate degree holders both in Texas and nationally, along with trends in state licensing and employer job postings.

Given the increased demand expected for graduate degrees, policymakers may want to also understand if the new estimated demand is large or small. To help facilitate a broader understanding of graduate education demand in the Texas labor market, we also considered demand in three other states: California, Florida, and New York. We used each state's occupational employment projections over the 2012–22 period.[4]

For the comparative analysis, we did not specifically estimate graduate demand. Rather we converted the top occupational groups shown above into the closest general occupational groupings available in the data. We then obtained the percentage change in demand for each of these groupings for Texas, the three other states, and the country as a whole. Because of variation in the population of the four states and the size of occupations within them, we focused on percentage changes.

Table 3.1 shows how demand for these occupational groups in Texas compares across states and to the national average. The table shows that employment demand for workers within these occupational groups

4 For Florida, the employment projections were over 2015–23; as such we computed annual growth rates to estimate the ten-year change in occupational employment.

(and indeed in occupations in general) will grow quite rapidly in Texas relative to the other states and nationally.

The rapid employment demand growth projected in Texas suggests that strong population growth, along with a corresponding growth in sectors such as education and healthcare, is putting upward pressure on the demand for graduate-trained workers. The rise of the technology sector in areas such as Dallas and Austin could also be affecting growth for computer occupations, while the strong presence of the oil and gas industry across Texas translates into an increased demand for engineers.

Table 3.1. *Percentage Increase in Demand for Occupational Groups Linked to Graduate Demand across States, 2012–22*

Occupational Group	TX	CA	FL	NY	National
Healthcare	28.0	18.6	23.0	16.5	21.5
Engineers	25.8	12.4	14.4	8.7	8.6
Postsecondary Faculty	25.1	10.0	20.7	5.8	10.4
Computer	24.3	23.7	18.5	17.4	17.7
Teachers	22.3	16.1	23.6	16.5	16.6
Lawyers	21.1	10.9	16.5	7.3	9.3
Business	20.8	14.7	16.0	11.2	9.6
All Occupations, Regardless of Education Level	**21.3**	**14.9**	**15.9**	**11.1**	**10.8**

SOURCE: RAND calculations from BLS and state workforce data.

Growth of Texas Degree Production

We also examined graduate degree production by broad field to understand if Texas's recent growth in graduate degree production signals a potential for the state to match future demand. Figure 3.2 indicates the number of graduate degrees for Texas in 2005 and 2014 for broad fields. These fields were derived manually from more granular descriptions. For example, philosophy and religious studies degrees were categorized as liberal arts. These fields do not map directly to the labor market data above but in some cases can be compared directly to the occupational groups shown previously.

The chart highlights that Texas's increased graduate degree production since 2005 has mainly been in business and health fields. Graduate degree production in business fields grew by about 48 percent and in health fields by about 75 percent. These growth rates exceed the historical growth of Texas employment in the related occupational groups: 30 percent and 35 percent, respectively, on a ten-year basis. Nonetheless, the strong projected demand shown for the related occupational groups in Figure 3.1 may indicate a continued need for growth in business and health graduate degrees. The only field that did not experience growth is legal, which had a 6 percent reduction in degrees awarded. Given the widespread reports of low demand for lawyers discussed previously, that decrease seems like a reasonable response to demand in the occupation.

We also assessed total graduate degree completions for each field across our comparison states. Graduate degree growth in business and healthcare are comparable across all states. By contrast, in education, Texas increased its production by 30 percent while New York and Florida had declining degree completions over the same time period (Figure 3.3).

As we showed earlier, demand for graduates in education fields is expected to increase in Texas, so it is reassuring to see that Texas has been increasing its production of education graduate degrees faster than the other states. However, in engineering, Texas's growth is far behind New York, Florida, and California. Graduate engineering degrees in Texas grew by 21 percent over the ten-year period we examined but grew by 67 percent in New York, 62 percent in Florida, and 40 percent in California (Figure 3.4). Texas's low growth rates in engineering are all the more concerning because engineering jobs have been growing strongly in Texas (an estimated 30 percent in ten years) and are projected to grow two to three times as fast as these other three states according to the data presented in Table 3.1.

These findings indicate that while Texas may be ready to meet the future demand for business and health, its production of engineers may not be adequate. More detail on the total graduate degree completions for each field across our comparison states, and growth rates, is presented in Appendix Tables A.3 and A.4.

Figure 3.2. *Graduate Degree Completions by Broad Field, 2005 and 2014*

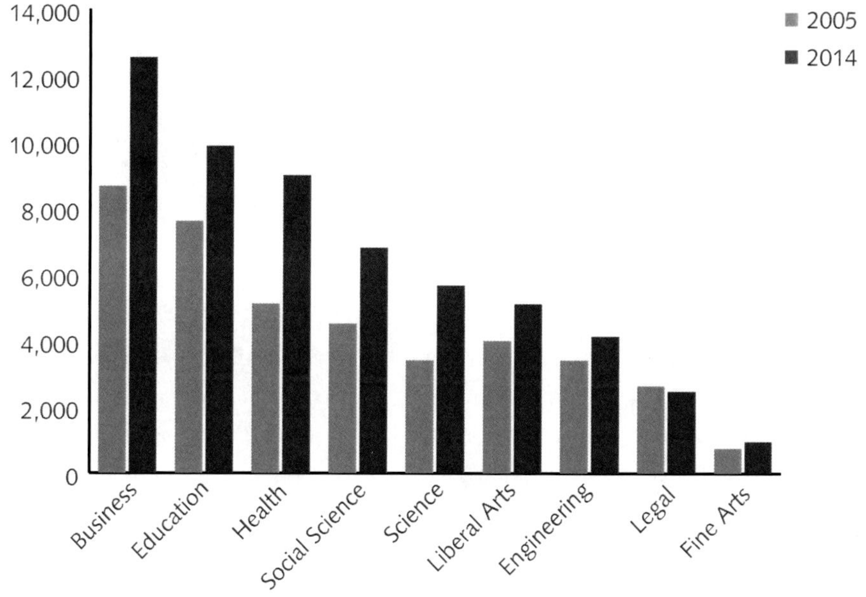

SOURCE: RAND calculations from IPEDS data.

Figure 3.3. *Graduate Degree Completions in Education by State*

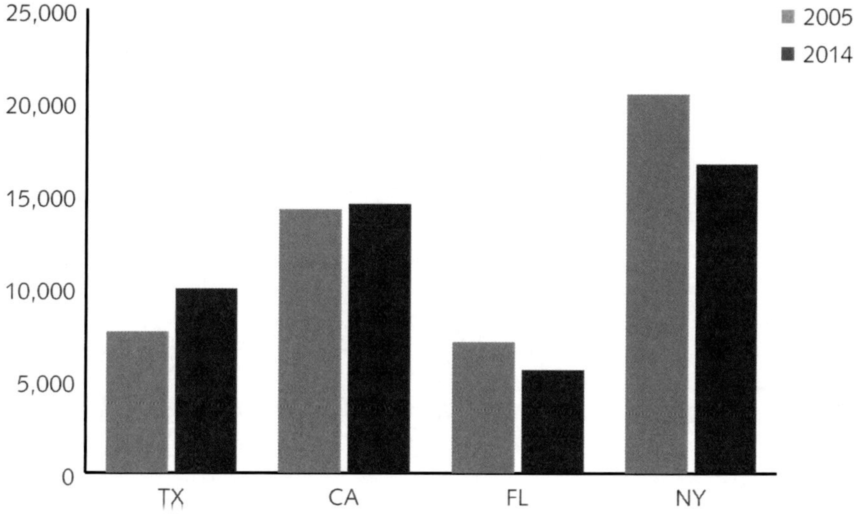

SOURCE: RAND calculations from IPEDS data.

Figure 3.4. *Graduate Degree Completions in Engineering by State*

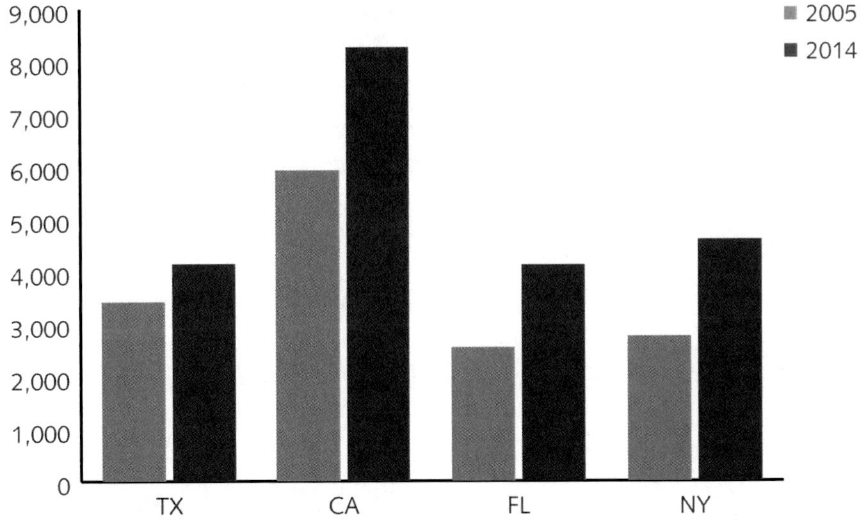

SOURCE: RAND calculations from IPEDS data.

Racial/Ethnic Composition of Graduate Degree Recipients

Texas has a large, diverse population, with especially fast growth in its Hispanic residents. Graduate degree production, however, does not fully represent Texas's diverse population. Figure 3.5 compares the racial/ethnic distribution of 2014 public institution graduate degree recipients (as a fraction of those who are citizens or permanent residents) to the general Texas population of 18- to 64-year-olds in that year. While whites and Asian-Americans are overrepresented in graduate degree awards, Hispanics are significantly underrepresented. In 2014, about 18 percent of graduate degree recipients were Hispanic, which is about half of the 36 percent share that the group has in the general 18- to 64-year-old population in Texas. As Texas's population grows and becomes more diverse, building representation of minorities in graduate education will be an ongoing challenge for the education ecosystem.

Figure 3.5. *Percentage Race/Ethnicity Distribution of Public University Graduate Degree Recipients and General Population (18- to 64-Years-Old) in Texas, 2014*

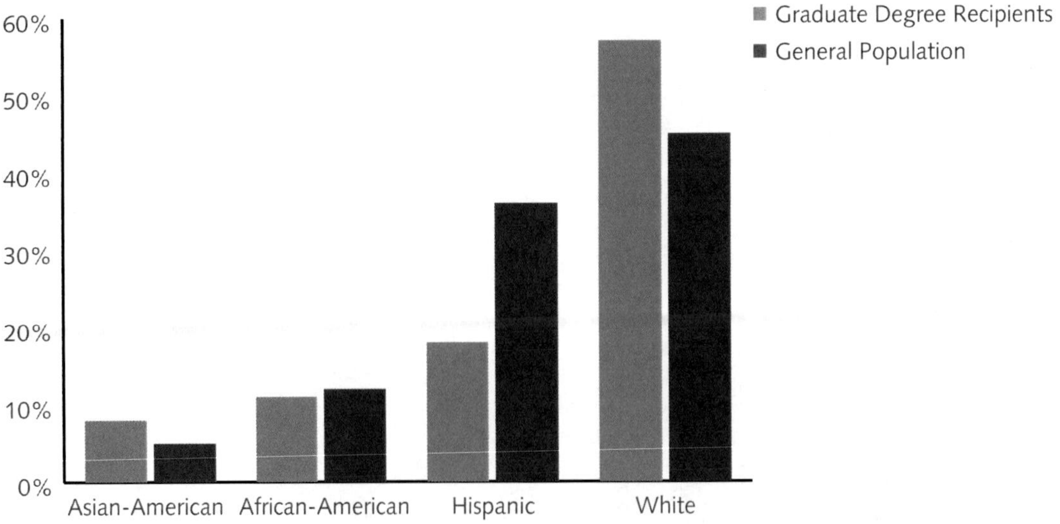

Note: Smaller racial groups omitted.

SOURCE: IPEDS and Current Population Survey.

At the broad field level, Hispanics are represented at fairly similar levels across most fields, with the exceptions of education and liberal arts, where Hispanics represent about 24 percent of graduate degrees awarded, somewhat closer to their overall share of the 18- to 64-year-old population of 36 percent.

Summary

Based on our analysis, we expect Texas to have strong demand for graduate degrees in the next ten years and beyond. The top occupational groups are expected to be business, healthcare, education, computers, and engineers. Generally, Texas has been increasing its production of graduate degrees in fields corresponding to these, although growth in engineering has been slow compared to other states and to projected demand. Texas's diverse population presents a challenge for the higher education ecosystem, with low Hispanic representation in graduate degrees awarded.

Minerva Studio/Fotolia

4 Texas's Position in Graduate Education and Research

Now that we have examined historical trends to estimate the ways that Texas's higher education ecosystem might meet a relatively straightforward concept of labor market demand, we turn to some broader considerations. While trained graduates represent an immediate output of higher education, in this chapter we look at broader and longer-term outcomes shown in the logic model of Figure 2.1, including workforce development, research performance, and institutional prestige. All of these outcomes are related to Texas's competitiveness in terms of attracting employers, especially in innovative industries that demand a base of R&D, including a graduate-trained workforce. As in the previous chapter, we compared Texas to California, Florida, and New York to illuminate Texas's standing relative to other large states.

This chapter offers a brief overview of the organization of higher education in these three comparison states. It then provides an overview of selected indicators that highlight the accomplishments of Texas higher education over the past ten years compared with the higher education sector in these states. For each comparison, we examined data over a ten-year period to understand the relative trends for each state and across states. The chapter concludes with suggested strategies that Texas can use to raise its competitive position, if desired.

State Systems for Higher Education

As we discuss in Chapter 1, Texas has an unusually complex organization for public higher education. It has six public university systems, four nonaffiliated universities, and additional systems for technical and community colleges. By contrast, none of the other three states we examined have more than two university systems. Texas's university systems are also not differentiated according to mission profile; the systems typically include institutions ranging from research-intensive to primarily teaching universities.

California operates under a Master Plan for Higher Education, which differentiates three systems of public higher education according to mission profile. The University of California (UC) system operates ten research universities, which are authorized to offer all degrees through the Ph.D. The California State University (CSU) system operates 23 campuses, which focus on undergraduate education, master's degrees, and doctorates in professional fields. CSU campuses can only propose Ph.D. programs jointly with a UC campus in fields that are not already offered by the UC campus. (Only about ten of these have been approved as of 2016.) California no longer has a state coordinating board for higher education, and according to our interviews with system officials, there is little state-level oversight. Each university system operates and has jurisdiction over degree offerings as dictated by the state's Master Plan. The Master Plan also establishes the California Community College system, which operates community colleges that grant associate degrees.

Florida has two public systems: the Florida State University system and the Florida College System (FCS). The Florida State University system consists of 12 universities that provide undergraduate and graduate degrees, with oversight from the Florida Board of Governors. These universities range from research universities to primarily teaching institutions. FCS includes 28 community colleges, which offer associate degrees and selected bachelor's degrees. FCS is overseen by the State Board of Education.

New York also has two public systems—the State University of New York (SUNY) with 64 campuses and the City University of New York (CUNY) with 19 campuses. Each has its own governing board and administration. However, the State Board of Regents, along with the State Department of Education, has authority over both university systems. Both SUNY and CUNY encompass a wide range of universities, including research universities and teaching universities. Each of the two systems also includes community colleges.

Growth of Graduate Degrees

Initially, we analyzed graduation data to understand the relative growth in graduate and professional degree production across Texas and the comparison states. Figure 4.1 indicates that Texas has grown its graduate degree production by more than 41 percent over the ten-year period from 2005 to 2014. This increase represents the largest percentage growth of any of the states analyzed. However, Texas still remains behind California and New York in total graduate degree production.

While Texas, California, Florida, and New York represent the four most populous states, their populations vary significantly. To contextualize graduate degree production by state, we examined per-capita degree production. Figure 4.2 on the next page indicates that when controlling for population size, Texas's production is comparable to California's production. Unlike the comparison states, the vast majority of Texas's graduate degree production is supplied by public institutions.

Figure 4.1. *Graduate and Professional Degree Production, 2005 and 2014*

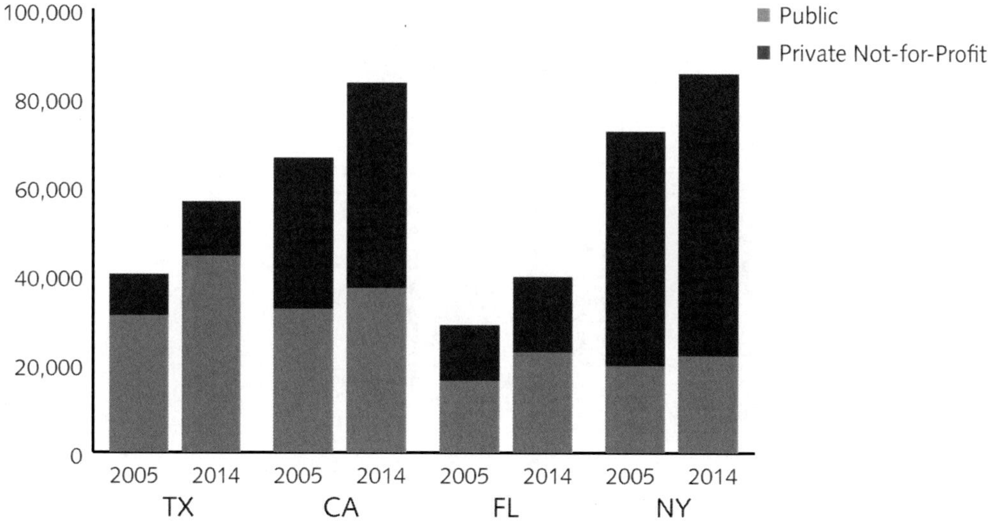

SOURCE: RAND calculations from IPEDS data.

Figure 4.2. *Per-Capita Graduate and Professional Degree Production, 2005 and 2014*

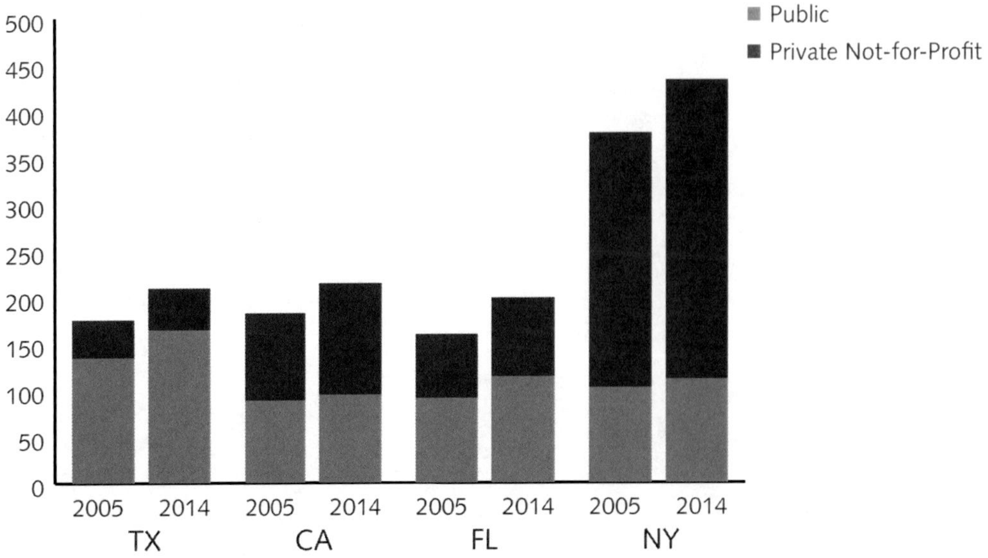

SOURCE: RAND calculations from IPEDS data.

Graduate Attainment

We also examined the overall graduate attainment rates for each state's population of 25- to 64-year-olds to understand how degree production is influencing the overall workforce. Figure 4.3 below indicates that while Texas's graduate attainment is growing, it remains behind comparison states.

Figure 4.3. *Percentage of Residents, 25- to 64-Years-Old, Holding a Graduate Degree, 2005 and 2012*

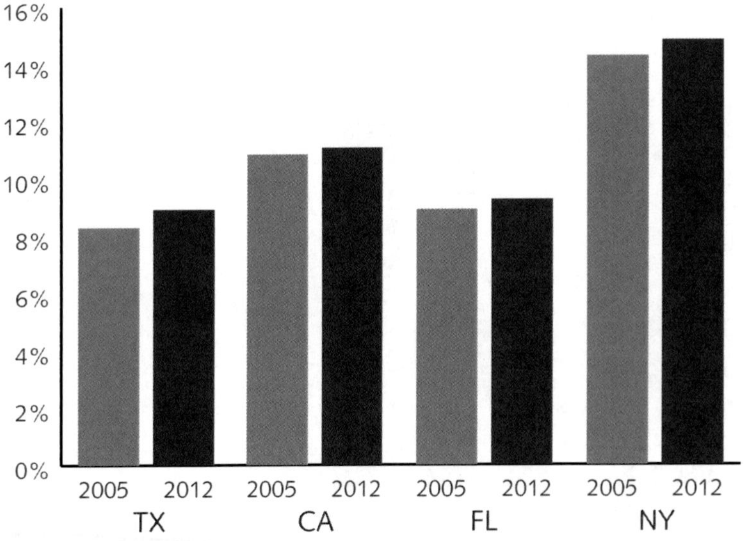

SOURCE: ACS tabulations.

Research

As the logic model in Figure 2.1 indicates, research is another primary output of higher education institutions. However, to conduct high-quality research, universities first need to secure funding. We examined the overall funding the federal government—the top funder of research for universities—has obligated to universities from 2004 to 2013 (latest data available) to better understand how Texas has performed in this area.

Figure 4.4 below shows the obligation trends over the ten-year period. It is important to note that overall federal funding for research was relatively flat over this time span, except for the 2009 stimulus funding. However, despite relatively stable overall funding, Texas's share of obligations has declined in recent years. In 2013, Texas received only 34 percent of the total level of funding provided to California. Adjusting for population differences, Texas reached about 49 percent of California's funding level, 44 percent of New York's, and 156 percent of Florida's.

Figure 4.4. *Federal Obligations to Higher Education for R&D, 2013*

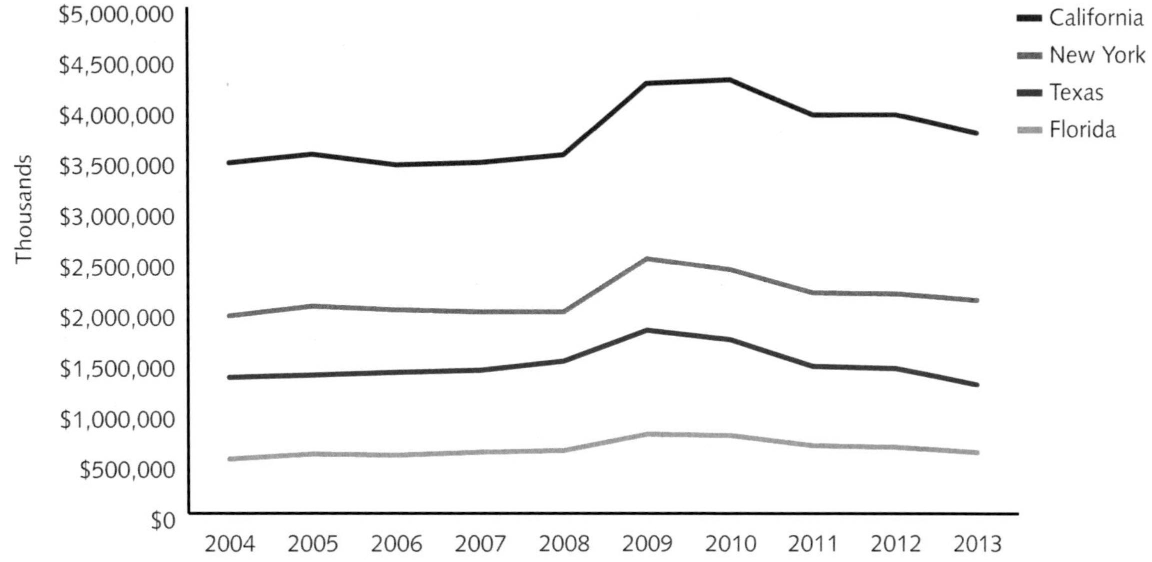

SOURCE: RAND calculations from National Science Foundation, National Center for Science and Engineering Statistics' Higher Education Research and Development Survey, Survey Cycle FY 2013.

To further understand research differences across states, we examined expenditures at the institutional level. The following four graphs (Figures 4.5–4.8) illustrate the 2013 expenditures for all institutions in each state that spent at least $50 million on research. For each state, we classified institutions as public, private, or health related. Health-related institutions are privately or publicly controlled organizations that focus solely on health-related education and research (e.g., independent medical schools). Institutions that currently include medical schools are indicated with an asterisk.[5]

Figure 4.5 indicates that in 2013, Texas had 17 institutions with research expenditures of more than $50 million and six with expenditures of more than $200 million a year. Of these six institutions, only two are general public universities—Texas A&M University and the University of Texas at Austin. The others are health-related institutions that have different funding resources and constraints than general universities. It is also important to note the significant difference in funding between the top two general public institutions and

5 The University of Texas at Austin welcomed its first class of medical students in 2016. Therefore, it is signified as having a medical school even though our analyses focus on 2013, which was before the institution had formally opened its medical school.

Figure 4.5. *Texas R&D Expenditures by Institution, 2013*

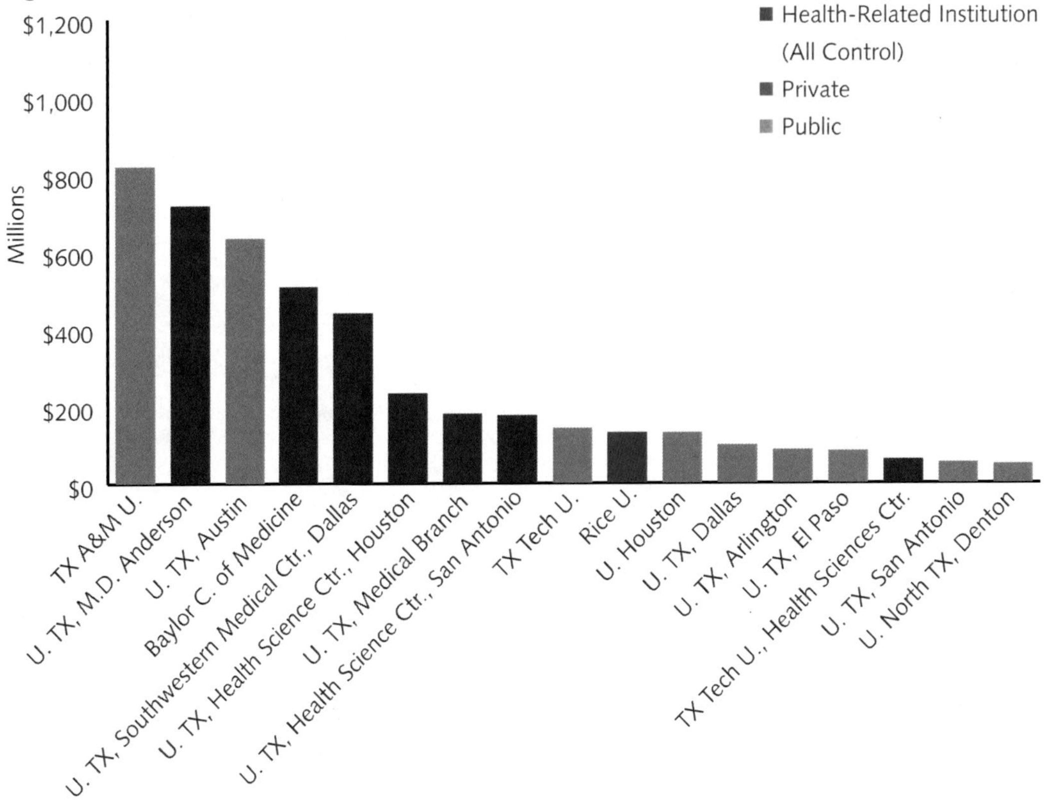

SOURCE: RAND calculations from National Science Foundation, National Center for Science and Engineering Statistics' Higher Education Research and Development Survey, Survey Cycle FY 2013.

the next set of public institutions. Texas Tech University spent only $83 million on research in 2013 while the University of Texas at Austin, the next highest general public institution, spent $643 million on research.

By comparison, California had 15 institutions with research expenditures of more than $50 million in 2013; 11 had expenditures of more than $200 million on research.[6] Of these 11 institutions, six are publicly controlled. Figure 4.6 also highlights the differences in institutional organization between the two states. While Texas has several institutions that are solely health related, until recently it has had no academic medical centers integrated with general academic campuses. By contrast, this integrated medical-general model is responsible for the majority of California's top research spending institutions.

Figure 4.7 illustrates the seven institutions in Florida that spent more than $50 million on research in 2013. While the graph indicates that Florida had a much smaller set of institutions that dedicate resources to research, it only had two fewer institutions than Texas with expenditures of more than $200 million on R&D.

Finally, Figure 4.8 indicates that New York had 16 institutions that spent more than $50 million on R&D in 2013 and 10 institutions that spent more than $200 million. The majority of these 10 institutions are privately controlled universities.

6 The UC Office of the President is not listed in Figure 4.6. However, it received $67 million in funding in 2013. These funds were distributed to its UC campuses, and therefore the office is not included as a separate institution.

Figure 4.6. *California R&D Expenditures by Institution, 2013*

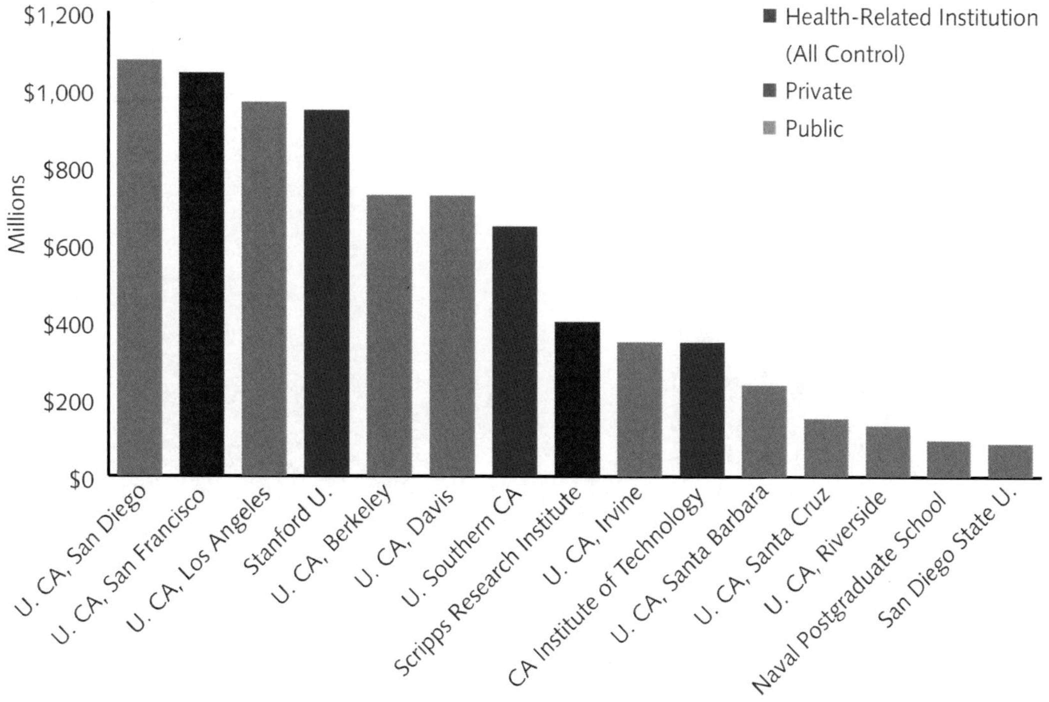

SOURCE: RAND calculations from National Science Foundation, National Center for Science and Engineering Statistics' Higher Education Research and Development Survey, Survey Cycle FY 2013.

Figure 4.7. *Florida R&D Expenditures by Institution, 2013*

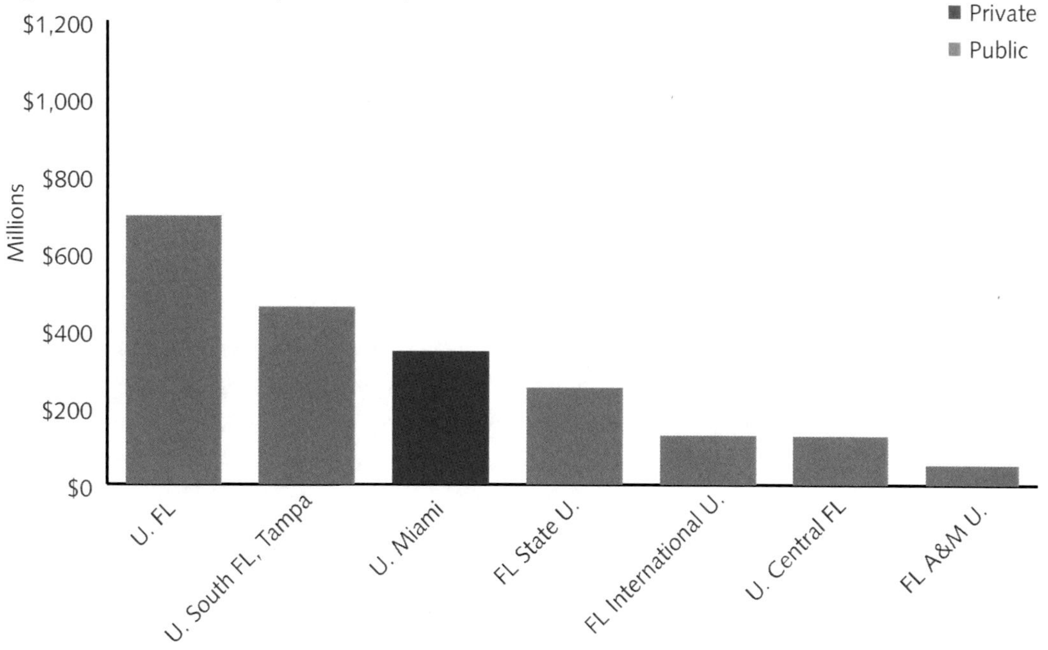

SOURCE: RAND calculations from National Science Foundation, National Center for Science and Engineering Statistics' Higher Education Research and Development Survey, Survey Cycle FY 2013.

Figure 4.8. *New York R&D Expenditures by Institution, 2013*

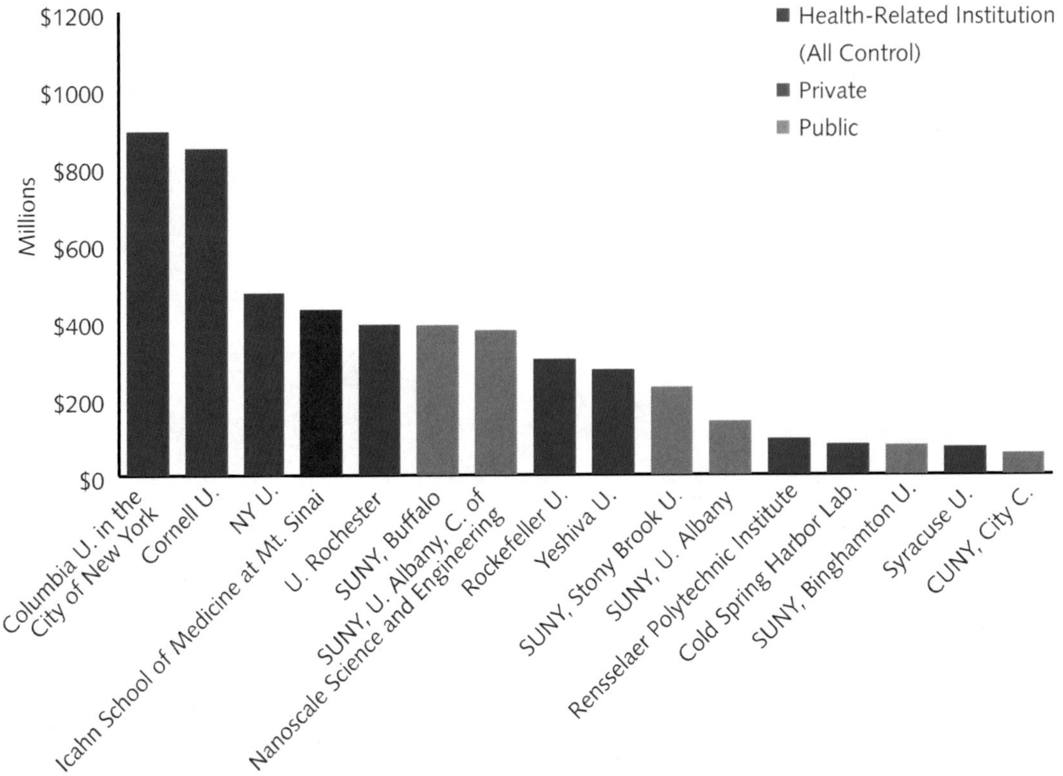

SOURCE: RAND calculations from National Science Foundation, National Center for Science and Engineering Statistics' Higher Education Research and Development Survey, Survey Cycle FY 2013.

In comparing research expenditures across states, Texas's health-related institutions clearly are a unique set of resources responsible for the majority of research in the state. However, Texas did not spend nearly the amount on research that California's top institutions did in 2013. This finding indicates that Texas has a long way to go if it wants to be on par with California in terms of research output. In addition, the declining share of research obligations from the federal government signals a potential concern for Texas.

Ranking

Institutional prestige is an outcome of higher education institutions' efforts to admit the brightest students and produce the greatest research. While graduate degree production and research funding are good signals of this ultimate outcome, directly measuring institutional prestige, where possible, is useful. Therefore, we analyzed two indicators of institutional prestige that universities commonly use in promoting their own organizations.

The Carnegie Classification of Institutions of Higher Education categorizes all U.S. universities on their research intensity if they award at least 20 research-focused doctoral degrees each year. This classification is conducted every five years and is based on the number of Ph.D. degrees awarded and sponsored research funding (assessed both in absolute terms and relative to the number of faculty at the institution). Carnegie classifies research-intensive institutions into three groups: Research 1 (R1)—highest research activity, Research 2 (R2)—higher research activity, and Research 3 (R3)—moderate research activity. R1 status is seen as a prestigious achievement that many universities aim to attain as it indicates a strong emphasis on research on par with the top universities in the United States.

Figure 4.9 indicates the number of institutions within each state that were classified as R1, R2, or R3 in 2005 and 2015. Texas significantly increased the number of its recognized research universities, growing from 16 to 25 in a ten-year period. This growth is the largest among the states we analyzed. The number of R1-recognized institutions grew from three to eight in Texas while California and New York saw no growth in R1 institutions over the same time period. This finding indicates that while federal research obligations are not growing for Texas overall, individual institutions have grown their research portfolios.

Figure 4.9. *Number of Carnegie Research Universities (R1, R2, and R3) by State, 2005 and 2015*

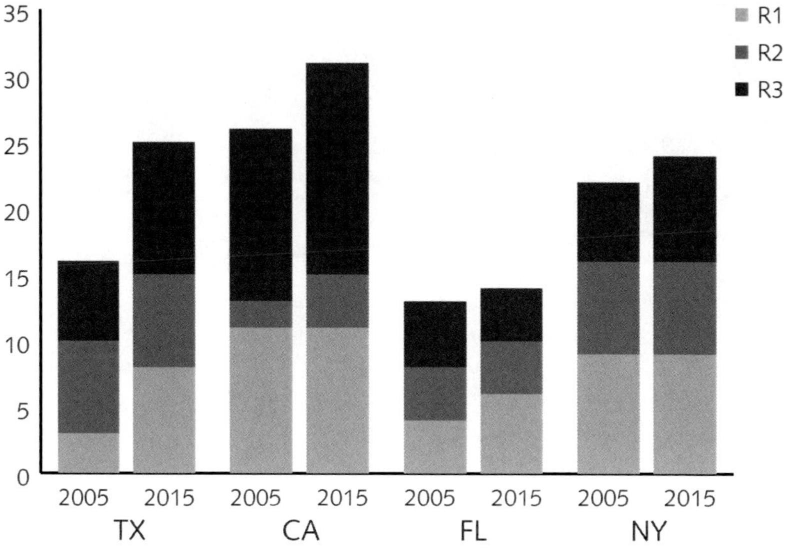

SOURCE: RAND calculations from Carnegie Classification, 2005 and 2015.

We also used ShanghaiRanking's Academic Ranking of World Universities to compare institutional prestige across states. ShanghaiRanking uses six objective metrics that focus on measuring research and graduate outputs to rank the top 500 institutions in the world. These metrics include "number of alumni and staff winning Nobel Prizes and Fields Medals, number of highly cited researchers selected by Thomson Reuters, number of articles published in journals of nature and science, number of articles indexed in Science Citation Index—Expanded and Social Sciences Citation Index, and per capita performance of a university."[7]

Figure 4.10 indicates the number of universities in each state that were listed in the top 500 according to ShanghaiRanking in 2005 and 2015. Given the lack of growth in top universities across all the states, we also looked at the trend for the United States as a whole. Overall, the number of ranked U.S. universities dropped 13 percent over the ten-year period. This drop indicates escalating international competition. However, Texas and Florida each lost only one institution.

7 About Academic Ranking of World Universities. Website: http://www.shanghairanking.com/aboutarwu.html. Last accessed 8/12/2016.

Figure 4.10. *Number of Institutions Ranking in Top 500 of ShanghaiRanking by State, 2005 and 2015*

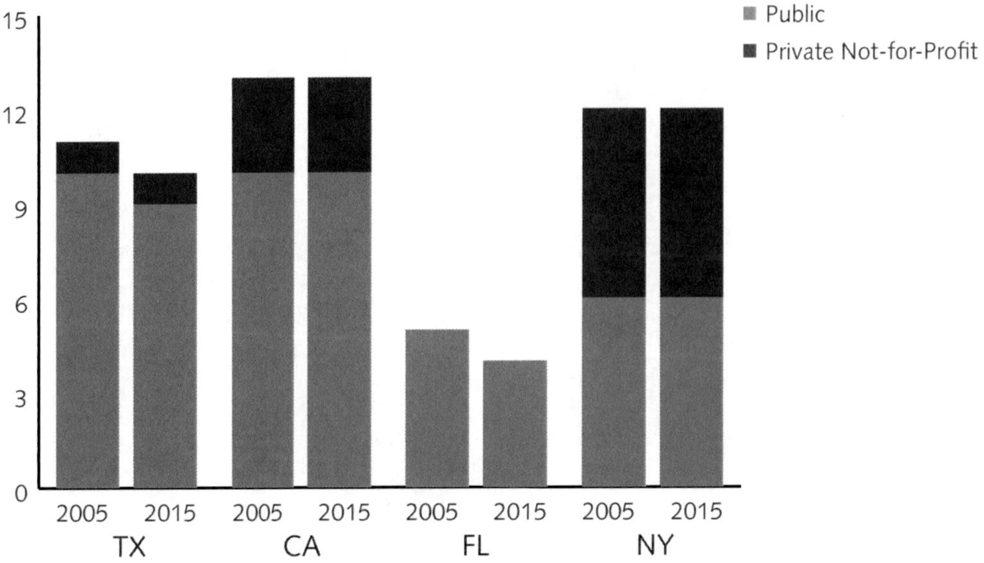

SOURCE: Academic Ranking of World Universities.

Of the ten Texas universities in the top 500 in 2015, only four institutions were ranked in the top 100. By contrast, 11 of California's 13 ranked universities were in the top 100. New York had four in the top 100, and Florida had one. This result indicates that while Texas is broadly competitive internationally, competition is increasing, and Texas has less representation at the most-competitive levels compared to California.

Strategies for Raising Competitiveness

Texas's position compared to other states and countries is important to its state competitiveness. The ranking indicators we presented previously show that Texas is increasing its number of Carnegie-recognized research universities at a fast rate but, especially compared to California, is not represented at the highest levels of international competition and does not attract the same share of federal research funding. If Texas desires to further increase the competitiveness of its universities, it will likely need additional investments in research capacity.

Research universities benefit from a concentration of resources and deliberate strategies to invest in research activity (see Brewer, Gates, and Goldman, 2002; Salmi, 2009). Since California separates public universities into two systems based on mission, it can direct higher levels of funding to the research-intensive UC campuses compared to the CSU campuses. Texas, on the other hand, allocates funding for education based on semester credit hours, broad field, and level of education but with no higher funding rates based on the research mission of certain campuses. Instead, Texas provides some state funding specifically based on research activity, recognizing that public universities need investments in research programs to promote excellence.

In 2015, the Texas legislature restructured state research investment programs to align them more clearly with THECB's peer groups and to concentrate funding on the campuses with the highest research activity. Table 4.1 provides an overview of the current programs including eligibility and funding.

We found that the basic design of these programs is sound in aiming to increase the research capacity of Texas public institutions. The programs generally concentrate additional state resources on institutions that have already developed a measure of success in building research programs. Furthermore, they allocate funding based on measured performance in attracting research funding or, in the case of the Governor's University Research Initiative (GURI), to campuses that can attract world-class researchers from out of state.

Table 4.1. *Texas State Research Funding Programs*

Program	Target Institutions	Description	Funding (FY 16 & 17)
Texas Research Incentive Program (TRIP)	Emerging Research Institutions	Matching funds to leverage private gifts for research and faculty recruitment.	$138,097,074
Texas Research University Fund (TRUF)	Research Institutions	Funds based on three-year average of total R&D expenditures to support faculty at institutions with more than $450 million in R&D expenditures.	$147,075,794
Core Research Support Fund (CRSF)	Emerging Research Institutions	Funds based on total and restricted R&D expenditures to support faculty and their labs at emerging research institutions.	$117,111,410
Texas Comprehensive Research Fund (TCRF)	Other (Nonresearch and Nonemerging Research Institutions)	Funds based on restricted R&D expenditures to support faculty and their labs at nonresearch-based institutions.	$14,272,388
National Research University Fund (NRUF)	Selected Emerging Research Institutions	Funds to emerging research universities that expended more than $45 million on restricted research for two years in a row.	$37,817,288
Autism Research Centers Program	Any	Funding to autism research centers to support parent-direct treatment, board-certified behavioral analyst training, and R&D.	$8,100,000
Cancer Prevention and Research Institute of Texas (CPRIT)	Any	Matching funding for grants to institutions and medical research facilities to support cancer research.	$600,110,000
Governor's University Research Initiative (GURI)	Any	Matching funding to institutions to support recruiting Nobel Laureates and National Academy members from outside institutions.	$40,000,000

SOURCE: THECB (2015b).

Recommendations

To enhance the competitiveness of Texas public higher education institutions, continue, and consider increasing, state research program funding. To continue to build the competitiveness of Texas public institutions, the state should continue its research funding programs and may wish to consider increasing their funding. Such increased funding could provide a greater match rate to campuses, further accelerating the development of research infrastructure on campuses that have shown some success in building nationally competitive research programs.

To enhance institutional ability to recruit key researchers from other states, consider more flexibility in the GURI. Specifically with regard to the GURI, representatives of some emerging research universities with low endowments stated that while they might be able to attract notable out-of-state researchers who would qualify for this funding, they did not have sufficient flexible funds (like endowment income) to meet the local matching requirement with nonstate funds. The state may wish to consider a more flexible approach to matching requirements that allows a broader selection of universities the opportunity to attract these researchers to Texas.

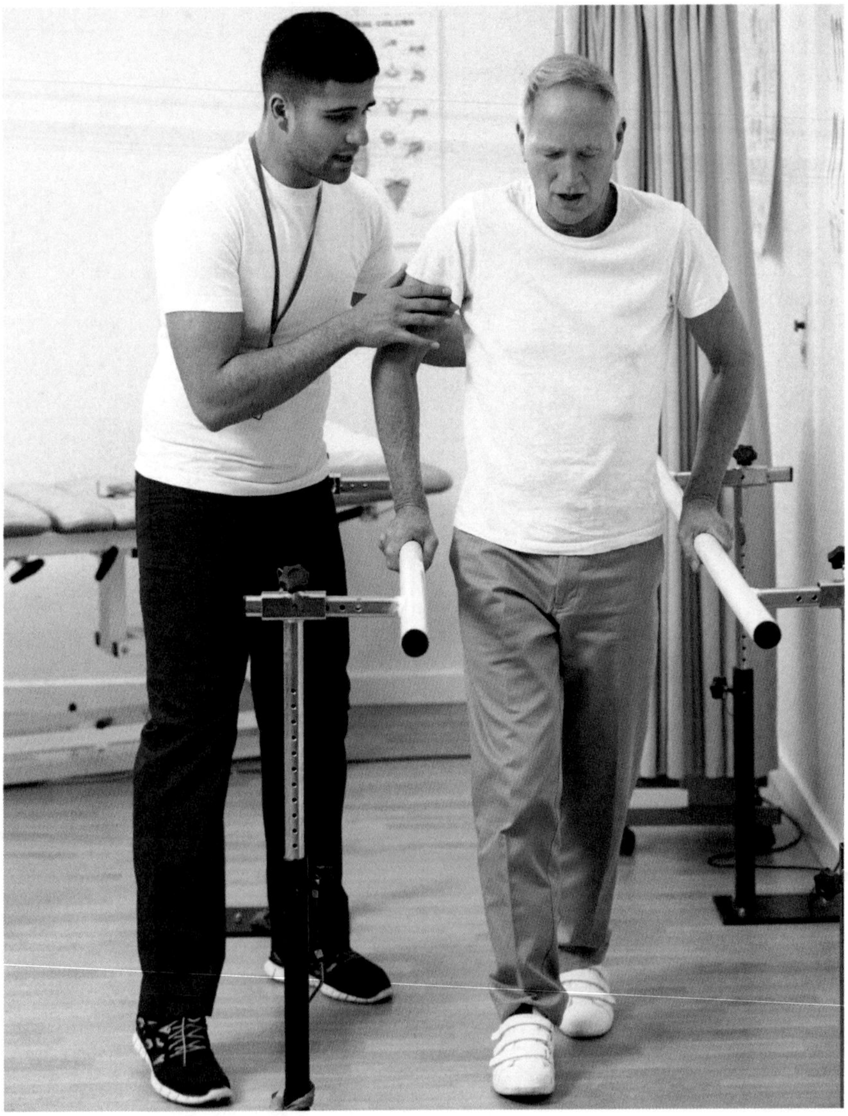

Monkey Business/Fotolia

5 Graduate Program Decisionmaking Process

The previous chapters have established that Texas is likely to need substantial continued expansion of its graduate programs. Some of this expansion can come from increasing enrollments in existing programs, but some will likely come from new programs. Developing new programs presents the state and institutions with both opportunities and challenges. In this chapter, we explore the process that institutions use to make decisions about graduate program development to provide recommendations for managing the expansion process most effectively.

We first describe a framework underlying the decisionmaking process for expanding graduate programs. This framework was developed based on our synthesis of the case study findings. We then discuss in detail a set of motivators or factors that drive institutions to propose new graduate programs, which we derived from the framework. Then we discuss the main points stakeholders raised in our case study interviews that align with each motivator. When applicable, we highlight whether the motivators apply to specific graduate programs or fields. We also discuss how each motivator could inform improvements in THECB's review process for graduate programs and recommend actions that THECB, the state, or higher education institutions could take to improve the decisionmaking process for expanding graduate programs.

Framework Depicting the Decisionmaking Process for Proposed Graduate Programs

In this section, we describe briefly the process institutions use to make decisions regarding expanding their graduate programs. This framework is derived from the case study findings and lays the foundation for identifying factors that motivate institutions to propose new programs (discussed in depth in the next section). At the center of the framework is an institution's decision to expand or not to expand graduate programs (see Figure 5.1). Both external factors (in grey) and internal factors (in purple) inform decisions to expand graduate programs. External factors include labor market needs for graduates with specific skills at the state and national levels, as well as student demand for specific graduate programs. Institutions are likely to expand their graduate programs in certain fields if employers demand them to fill openings for professions in these fields or as an entry to certain professions. How institutions respond to employer demand or preferences is confounded by institutions' culture and internal politics. Furthermore, labor market demand is not sufficient. There also has to be student demand for the proposed graduate programs; otherwise the programs will have low enrollment and will result in loss of institutional resources. The extent to which established graduate programs within a field are competing with each other also informs the program decision. Institutions are more likely to propose new graduate programs in contexts where competition is low.

Figure 5.1. *Process Used by Texas Institutions When Considering New Graduate Degree Programs*

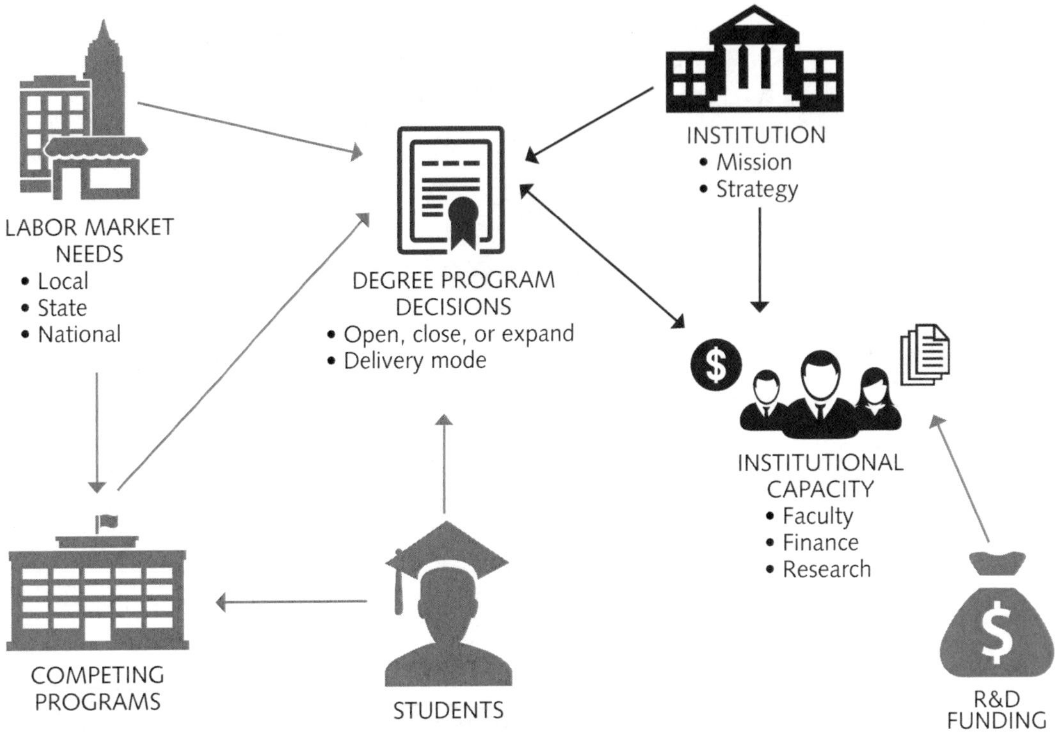

SOURCE: Authors' analysis of case study data.

Factors internal to the institution also shape its decision to pursue new graduate programs. An institution that views itself as an education institution is less likely to pursue Ph.D. programs than an institution that considers creating new knowledge its primary mission. Similarly, faculty research capacity and research resources play critical roles in the institution's decision to expand graduate programs. An institution with limited capacity or federal research funds is less likely to focus on expanding graduate programs that are research focused.

Beyond the internal and external factors depicted in Figure 5.1 that affect institution decisionmaking, the broader state context in which the institutions are embedded can either encourage or discourage graduate program expansion. First, in terms of structure and as discussed previously, higher education institutions in Texas can move among the six peer groups that vary in research intensity, if they meet the established criteria for each group. Institutional mobility in Texas is thus less static than in California and New York. For example, in California, institutions' expansion of research graduate programs is defined by the higher education system to which the institutions belong (UC or CSU), while New York state will not allow institutions with nonresearch missions to expand their research graduate programs unless their mission is changed and approved by the Board of Regents. The fact that Texas allows institutions to move across peer groups might encourage institutions to expand Ph.D. programs.

Second, unlike California, Texas has a board that oversees higher education institutions. THECB sets new policies, defines the criteria for approving new graduate programs, and reviews new program proposals submitted by the institutions. Thus, in Texas, institutional decisions to expand graduate programs are informed by the strategic planning and criteria set by THECB. THECB's recently adopted statewide *60x30TX* strategic plan will require significant expansion of higher education by 2030. This state policy might further mobilize institutions to expand their graduate programs to ensure that they are producing the needed numbers of graduates, including faculty to staff expanding institutions. Similarly, institutions might emphasize some specific fields over others when expanding graduate programs in response to the criteria established by THECB.

Factors Motivating Institutions to Propose Graduate Programs: Findings and Recommendations

This section discusses motivators of graduate program expansion at the institutional level rather than the contextual or state level. Thus, we examine external and internal factors delineated in the framework and derive a number of motivators that lead institutions to propose new graduate programs. Some motivators are concerned with the positioning of the institution (as a whole or within specific fields) in relation to other institutions. Other motivators are related to expanding specific graduate programs, without a primary focus on institutional positioning. For example, an institution might decide to expand its graduate degrees in a specific department or program in response to student or labor market demand, increased competition among graduate programs within the field, or new requirements set by professional organizations. Thus, we classify the motivators across a continuum, representing different levels at the institution (Figure 5.2). Prestige-seeking motivators are institutional-level motivators because they are concerned with institutional standing and how an institution views and understands its mission. Other motivators are considered to be closer to the departmental level as they are concerned with advancing specific graduate programs.

Figure 5.2. *Institutional Motivators for New Graduate Degree Programs*

Seeking Research-Intensive Status

The institutions in this study reported a number of reasons for seeking research-intensive status. A common motivation is to improve their positioning and ranking to attract better faculty and better academically prepared students, as well as increase their competitiveness in securing external research funding.

Another reason for seeking research-intensive status is to be responsive to state needs. Some of the institutions we interviewed highlighted the fact that there are a limited number of public institutions in Texas at the highest national levels of research activity. They argued that this number is inadequate for meeting the needs of the student population in Texas who are interested in attending research programs (such as Ph.D. programs) and that a significant number of students located in large geographic areas, including rural areas, are left out from pursuing research graduate degrees because they have no access to a major research university. These students have resource constraints prohibiting them from relocating to attend the few universities that have research programs. Some of the institutions interviewed viewed themselves as having a responsibility of becoming research intensive to provide these students with access and opportunities to pursue research graduate degrees.

Finally, a few study institutions reported seeking research-intensive status because they belong to a university system that they perceive as being research focused. However, this view is not aligned with how university systems are structured in Texas, where each system consists of universities with varying degrees of research level and not all universities within a system are expected to have high levels of research activity. These few institutions, however, argued otherwise and indicated that their research mission is defined by the fact that they belong to a research university system.

PointImages/Fotolia

Even when institutions are motivated to become research intensive, they indicated that capacity is a major determinant in the decision to pursue research-intensive status. Specifically, they reported not seeking such status or not even proposing Ph.D. programs if they do not have faculty with some research capacity or a body of research work that is concentrated and has potential to grow in a specific field.

Institutions that are motivated to become research intensive but do not have current capacity engage in efforts over many years to build capacity. Interviewees at study institutions seeking research-intensive status reported taking slow but deliberate approaches over many years. Their desire to be research intensive is built into their strategic plan. Further, their efforts are focused on building on their institutional roots and strengths and over time transforming specific pockets of research to research across all fields and disciplines taught at the university. These institutions are using competitive salaries to attract tenured faculty who have existing grants and labs and have a history of bringing in grant funding. They are also slowly attracting new junior faculty who are trained as researchers. The institutions are providing them with startup packages so that they can focus on research. In addition to increasing research productivity, one of the goals for hiring junior faculty is to change the culture of the institution and slowly transform the expectation of faculty as senior faculty retire. That is, institutions that have a teaching mission and are aspiring to become research intensive are hiring different types of new faculty compared to the teaching faculty they used to hire. These new faculty have research capacity and are hired with the expectation that they will engage in research activities and over time bring in research money through grants. In the long run faculty with research capacity will outnumber previously hired faculty that mostly focus on teaching. This evolution will lead the institution from a teaching-focused culture to a research-focused culture. Since this cultural transformation is a slow process, some institutions indicated that at least for the short term they would have two tracks: a research faculty track and a teacher faculty track with a higher course load. The long-term goal is to ultimately have all faculty engage in research and have that reflected in changes in promotion and tenure policies.

Seeking to Grow the Research Agenda in a Specific Field

Our interviews also demonstrate that some institutions seek to increase their research capacity and prominence but do not necessarily aspire to become research-intensive universities. They view research as a way to enhance the academic environment experienced by students, including undergraduate students. That is, faculty engagement in research creates new knowledge that can be shared with undergraduate students as part of instruction. These institutions place their efforts in concentrated areas, such as expanding their strong undergraduate programs to the graduate level or developing graduate programs in areas in which faculty members have built a body of knowledge around a specialization. These graduate programs tend to be distinctive and tightly linked to local context, including local industry. For example, in the coastal area there is an energy industry. Some of the engineering and GIS graduate programs in that area are very specialized and are linked to that industry.

Recommendations

As discussed in Chapter 4, Texas may wish to increase the number of public research universities that are nationally and internationally competitive. However, there are challenges associated with institutional movement. One challenge is that such a movement might lead to changes in the mission of the institution and affect student access, especially since institutional ranking takes into account undergraduate admission and selectivity. In fact, our interviews revealed that one institution seeking research-intensive status had changed its open access policy to a selective policy that accepts the top 25 percent of Texas students in its undergraduate programs. This change is understandable since the institution will need to attract students who are better prepared academically. But it also means that a large group of students who are regional and who traditionally were eligible for admission are blocked from attending this institution under the new policy. Another challenge is that the pressure to become a research-intensive institution may lead to the expansion of graduate programs that are not essential in meeting student or labor market demand, such as academic Ph.D. programs. This is because to become research intensive, an institution would need to have a large number of Ph.D. programs covering multiple disciplines. Institutions might establish such programs even if there is not a clear need for them in Texas's labor market.

We provide two recommendations pertaining to institutional positioning and expanding research agendas. The first relates to proposal review, and the second addresses a broader issue related to changes in institutional mission and student access.

Place more emphasis on institutional support and policies in reviewing doctoral program proposals. THECB requires all institutions to provide a link to their strategic plan when they are proposing new doctoral programs. A strategic plan articulates institutions' long-term activities, which signify whether institutions are planning to maintain their current group classification or have plans to move up the classifications. Although THECB currently considers the institution's strategic plan in its review of doctoral program proposals, it could place more emphasis on links between proposed doctoral research programs and the availability of institutional support for research as well as institutional policies conducive to research. For example, THECB could place more weight on research capacity at the institutional level, not just at the level of the department in which the program would be housed. Institutions with research capacity can provide a broad base of resources and financial support to help ensure program success. THECB could also place more weight on policies pertaining to faculty workload, release from teaching, and other related issues that facilitate faculty engaging in research activities.

If the doctoral program changes the institution's strategic plan or direction, THECB could require the institution to make changes to its strategic plan first to embody and support the proposed doctoral program. However, it is important that THECB not systematically exclude institutions from expanding into doctoral education, or expanding their doctoral offerings, provided the institutions have supportive missions, strategies, resources, and policies.

Review student access regularly and consider alternative pathways when needed. Although institutions should be able to expand their research or Ph.D. programs, they and the state should also be sensitive to how such expansion could affect student admission to undergraduate programs. Although many institutions balance graduate education with good undergraduate opportunities and student access, others might find it more challenging to achieve such a balance. Institutions that are becoming more research intensive should put mechanisms in place early on to monitor any changes to access. For example, institutions or systems could periodically review any changes in student access. If changes in admission occur, we recommend that institutions and systems explore alternatives for how to serve students who would no longer be admitted. These options could include developing alternative pathways at the institution. Another option is to expand articulation with community colleges so that students who are not accepted under the new admission criteria could enroll first at the community college and then transfer to the institution during their junior year. Institutions could also identify ways to expand their own student population to encompass both better academically prepared students and their traditional local students or work with and support other institutions in the area to expand student education services and ensure that all students have the opportunity to receive a local college education. THECB could provide general guidelines on how institutions could deal with student access issues if missions change.

Engaging in Positive Margin Activities

Another factor motivating the expansion of graduate programs is to generate positive operating margins that can be invested in activities that require subsidies. Our interviews indicate that expanding master's programs, especially nonresearch programs, is an activity that generates revenue, which is central to growing doctoral programs. Master's programs are a source of revenue for institutions because they are not expensive to operate and have lower costs per student. Master's programs are short in duration; have classes with large numbers of students; and often do not include extensive theses, which require faculty to spend additional time mentoring students. Further, in many fields, students at the master's level tend to be employed and do not expect full financial support. Institutions thus not only recover program costs through student tuition but also earn margins given the economies of scale of master's programs. According to the interviews, institutions use this source of revenue to invest in Ph.D. programs; in particular, revenues are used to fund competitive salaries to attract notable faculty and to provide financial support to doctoral students.

Our interviews also indicate that institutions have been increasingly providing master's programs online through partnerships with private companies, such as education publishing and assessment companies. Interviewees across the 12 institutions consistently indicated that online programs generate more revenue than face-to-face programs because of their scalability and potentially greater enrollment.

Online programs provide some advantages. They improve access to graduate education by overcoming geographical challenges for students, especially in certain locations where it may take students hours to get to the nearest university. Further, according to our interviews, in certain fields such as nursing, physical therapy, and education, students tend to be nontraditional. Online programs provide such students with flexibility to take the courses from any location and at any time (for online courses that are asynchronous).

It is important to note that some department leaders we interviewed expressed concerns about the quality of online programs. They indicated that the classes tend to be very large (e.g., more than 100 students) and that the professors of record are not necessarily the individuals teaching the class. The department leaders also expressed concerns about the extent to which private companies seeking to increase profitability could influence the structure of the online courses. One department leader reported that a private organization requested that the department's online programs be restructured to compete with similar programs for student enrollment. Specifically, the private provider asked the institution to make the online program accelerated and reduce the number of credits to attract adequate numbers of students so that both the institution and the private organization could benefit by generating positive margins. To reduce the number of credits the faculty eliminate a few topics from the program. One of the department leaders questioned whether an accelerated structure works for all students. This interviewee argued that students who do not have the same level of motivation or have other family responsibilities are likely to struggle in such a structure. According to the leaders of this specific program, no other modalities were available to students. This interviewee was also concerned whether course materials could be addressed in depth given that the course credit hours had been reduced.

Although master's programs are expanding considerably, our interviews indicate that most study institutions and departments do not require their master's programs to go through a program-level accreditation process to ensure that they are meeting specific standards for that subject matter. This lack of an accreditation process provides flexibility for institutions and private organizations to structure the master's programs in a way that maximizes their competitive edge and student enrollment, possibly without paying adequate attention to issues of program quality mentioned previously.

goodluz/Fotolia

Recommendations

A critical objective for expanding master's programs is to generate revenue that could be used for sustaining institutions generally and for strengthening and supporting doctoral programs specifically. This objective is not a concern as long as the master's programs are meeting workforce and student demand and their quality has not been compromised. Although some departments have master's program accreditation review, many do not.

Ensure the quality of master's programs through accreditation or an alternative process. While all graduate programs must be externally evaluated at least once every seven years, institutions may opt for a specific external review if the program is not accredited by a recognized body in the academic field. One option to ensure the quality of master's programs is for them to be accredited, if accreditation for the subject matter is offered by accrediting agencies. Another option is for institutions to implement a rigorous quality assurance process that uses independent experts to assess the quality of the programs on a set of criteria that are already established in the field. Obtaining accreditation or independent reviews by external experts is likely to improve how employers and prospective students view the legitimacy of the program, which in turn would increase an institution's competitive edge.

Develop THECB criteria for evaluating online master's program quality. THECB could also provide guidance to institutions on how to evaluate the quality of their online master's programs. Many online programs are approved as simple changes of delivery mode from existing face-to-face programs rather than undergoing a full proposal review. As a result, THECB does not have set criteria for evaluating online master's programs. However, over the past several years, the Learning Technology Advisory Committee (LTAC), an advisory committee assigned by THECB to engage in substantive and research discussions regarding learning technology, has reviewed THECB's rules and policies pertaining to doctoral distance education, revised the state's Principles of Good Practice in Distance Education, and researched critical issues in distance education. THECB could solicit LTAC assistance to derive criteria to help institutions evaluate their own online master's programs based on LTAC's review of online doctoral programs and overall research in distance learning. THECB and LTAC could also develop general criteria that would help institutions assess the quality of private partners, especially in aspects related to their role in program design and education delivery. Institutions could be involved in this process or asked to provide input regarding the criteria.

Competition

Competition among study institutions seems to be more prevalent than collaboration, though the competition varies by institution type. Research-intensive institutions tend to compete with similar universities both in Texas and nationwide. These institutions focus on expanding their Ph.D. programs to increase their competitiveness. That is, they engage in efforts that produce positive margins and increase research productivity for the purpose of generating adequate resources to propose new Ph.D. programs and attract and support high-quality faculty and doctoral students. Less-intensive research institutions tend to compete locally. Although these institutions also have Ph.D. programs, they concentrate their efforts on increasing their competitive edge at the master's and professional doctoral levels. For example, many of those institutions have moved from face-to-face instruction to providing online master's and professional doctoral degrees in education and health sciences. The goal is to compete for student enrollment against other institutions that have similar programs.

A few of the study institutions or departments within institutions kept their face-to-face mode of instruction, arguing that this mode ensures higher-quality education. They were able to keep the face-to-face mode of instruction delivery by offering satellite campuses to widen their geographic reach and accommodate student transportation needs.

To be competitive, some departments also differentiate their graduate programs from other programs through specialization. For some graduate programs, the specializations are legitimate, while for other programs their distinctiveness is symbolic. For example, one of the new doctoral programs that was discussed in our interviews and was considered distinctive by the institution offered courses that were similar to those offered in doctoral programs in other institutions.

Rob/Fotolia

In engineering, some institutions sought to increase the competitiveness of their graduate programs by offering work internships and training with employers in the industry. This feature is attractive to students because it provides opportunities for them to attain a job after they graduate with employers with whom they have interned.

We did identify several types of collaboration among institutions, but these collaborations primarily relied on the efforts of individual faculty within programs. For example, some faculty members engage with faculty from other institutions on research projects or serve on the dissertation or thesis committees of students from other institutions. In engineering, graduate programs tend to enroll a much higher proportion of international students than domestic students. (Interviews indicate that many domestic students have family responsibilities and prefer to work after they obtain their bachelor's degree because the industry pays them a similar salary to those with master's degree, at least in the early work years.) Thus, some engineering departments have developed pipelines between institutions to transition domestic students from undergraduate to graduate programs. These pipelines are not based on formal institutional articulation agreements but are instead mostly an understanding between departments from different institutions.

Finally, a small number of institutions reported partnering with other institutions within the same university system for a joint graduate program, although one institution would grant the degree. Usually this partnership includes an institution that has a particular research capacity and another institution that has less capacity. The goals for such collaboration are twofold: (1) Develop a graduate program to adequately meet labor market needs with respect to a specific field, and (2) build the research capacity of the less research-intensive institutions. In some cases, less research-intensive universities involved in such partnerships eventually terminated the relationship and established their own graduate programs. The termination of such relationships in some cases led to redundancy in graduate programs because of limited labor market needs, but in other cases separation was justified because of student and workforce demands.

Recommendation

Competition can be healthy and lead to innovative and high-quality programs, but it can also have a downside. Competition may generate program duplication if similar graduate programs are vying for students within the same geographic area. To keep the programs from closing down, institutions might change their standards to attract less academically prepared students, and the quality of the program might be affected. Furthermore, online programs, especially in education and some of the health sciences, tend to be similar and have no geographic boundaries, resulting in both increased competition for student enrollment and duplication. However, engineering online programs often do not face the same issues since these graduate programs attract international students and the supply of international students is greater compared to domestic students.

Avoid program duplication by promoting collaboration rather than competition at the system level. University systems could use their periodic meetings of provosts to discuss how to best manage competition among their campuses, reduce redundancy, and encourage healthy competition and collaboration. This recommendation does not mean that there should not be similar graduate programs within the same system or across systems. As long as there is student and workforce demand and the programs are of high quality and are serving various regions in Texas, programmatic duplication is not a problem. However, in instances where student and workforce demand are insufficient and not all institutions are equally equipped to implement high-quality research graduate programs, collaboration among institutions to provide graduate education benefits the institutions, system, and state. University systems could explore ways to incentivize collaboration. They also could provide resources and technical assistance to help institutions develop joint graduate programs that emphasize institutional strengths and build on their capacities. This type of institutional collaboration necessitates that system leaders promote thoughtful coordination to bring more value to each institution and not benefit one institution over another. Overall, it should help institutions use their limited resources most effectively.

Labor Market Demand

Meeting labor market needs is another motivator for proposing new graduate programs. Central to meeting those needs is examining where graduate degree holders work, in which occupations, and projections for these occupations. This examination provides a useful perspective on the labor force contributions of graduate degree holders. When institutions submit proposals to THECB for new graduate degree programs, they are required to provide data on related workforce factors such as indicators of unmet need.

All institutions have access to public data provided by BLS and TWC to measure workforce supply and demand. Institutions use these data sources, but not systematically. The datasets have shortcomings that might contribute to lack of steady use. First, they do not align specific degrees or certifications with occupations, which makes accurately estimating demand for proposed graduate programs difficult. Second, the datasets do not capture demand for emerging industries because these industries often have occupations not yet classified in state and national labor data. The data are also often too old to capture emerging trends.

Study institutions, thus, rely heavily on collecting qualitative data to build evidence to determine whether a new program is needed (or whether an existing program should be closed). Our interviewees reported that they engage in conversations with employers and industry experts and will typically place greater weight on this information than on statistical data. For example, some departments, specifically in health and science fields, have advisory boards that comprise prominent members in those industries. A major role of the advisory boards is to continually assess market needs and future trends and provide institutions with timely information regarding changes in the industry and workforce or skill needs. Other departments that have not established advisory boards have attempted to collect data on market demand and need through informal interviews with employers, their graduate students who are already working in the industry, and professional associations. One institution reported hiring a consultant to survey employers regarding labor market demand, and another indicated monitoring job postings to determine labor market needs. Irrespective of the methods used, all institutions reported using the qualitative information to help them identify the types of skills needed, and they integrate this information into the internal program development processes, during which department staff and faculty collaborate to structure the program and finalize curricula.

University administrators indicated that humanities disciplines are not linked to one occupation, and thus assessing their market demand is difficult. However, administrators did highlight the importance of humanities disciplines in preparing students for the workforce more generally because they develop transferrable skills. Furthermore, one interviewee emphasized that humanities disciplines are central to any university because humanities courses focus on developing critical thinking in all students. This interviewee advocated ensuring that there are enough Ph.D. programs in humanities to prepare future faculty to teach these courses at universities with different missions.

Although institutions engage in efforts to obtain information on labor market needs, the information obtained from employers tends to emphasize short-term needs because employers are interested in skills that match current job positions. Assessing long-term employer needs is challenging for institutions, and it is left largely up to university faculty to define the long-term skills to be promoted.

Interviewees suggest that institutions rarely track job placement of their graduates, which is critical for validating whether their programs are aligned with the labor market. One institution that tracks job placement of its Ph.D. graduates in the sciences was able to uncover the challenges Ph.D. students face in finding traditional positions in academia, while revealing opportunities for its graduates in nontraditional positions, including research and policy organizations. This finding has led the institution to begin exploring how it can modify its programs and institutional culture to meet market needs.

Although institution and department leaders agreed with the importance of obtaining job placement information, they indicated the need for resources to track job placement of their master's and professional doctoral degree holders due to their large numbers and the range of jobs they can obtain. Tracking Ph.D. graduates is easier because there are fewer occupation options.

Recommendations

Reliable employment forecasting is very challenging. Demand for new skills depends on a number of factors, including technological progress, government policies, and global conditions. However, institutions could improve their mechanisms for matching their graduate programs with workforce needs by engaging in ongoing research activities and surveying employers and graduates to assess demand for skills and the quality of graduates.

Support institutional access to labor market analysis tools. THECB currently encourages institutions to use BLS and TWC data to determine workforce needs when proposing new graduate programs. However, as mentioned earlier, the datasets do not map specific degrees to workforce data. Tools are available, such as those marketed by Economic Modeling Specialist International and Burning Glass, that make for simpler, systematic access to BLS and TWC data and also add real-time analysis of job postings. THECB could require institutions to use such tools to show evidence of workforce needs. To support institutions, THECB could acquire licenses to integrated labor market tools and provide institutions access to them. If acquiring a systemwide license is not feasible, THECB could explore obtaining a joint license with the institutions to lower costs.

Provide guidance on acceptable data sources beyond BLS and TWC. To capture labor market needs, institutions should follow traditional methods for data collection and analysis, including primary and secondary quantitative and qualitative data. THECB could support institutions by identifying some of the acceptable approaches for continually obtaining data from employers and increase institutional engagement with industry, which is somewhat lacking. For example, THECB could develop guidelines for how institutions could engage with employers or explore tools that have been designed to elicit regular employer input (e.g., those developed by the Center for Employability Outcomes at Texas State Technical College) and determine whether these tools can inform the development of graduate programs. THECB could also provide information on what tools are acceptable for emerging fields for which workforce commission data are not available yet.

THECB could also provide guidelines to institutions regarding the different individuals from whom to collect qualitative information when interacting with employers. For example, human-resource managers, high-level leadership, and industry experts may be better positioned to provide information on local employment and trends in demand, while first-line supervisors and employees in the positions can better speak to skill needs for occupations.

Provide education and training to ensure that data and tools are used wisely and effectively. THECB could help build institutions' capacity to identify workforce needs by providing training and workshops on how to use available workforce datasets, how to solicit pertinent workforce information, and how to interpret the resulting data.

Track graduate job placement. Finally, THECB could require institutions to track student job placements during the program review to see if the graduate programs have placed students in the labor market as intended. This requirement will signify to institutions the expectation to track this information and to invest in efforts to analyze labor market data more systematically. Institutions are likely to need additional resources to be able to track graduate student placement, especially at the master's level. The state could explore options for providing resources to the institutions.

Student Demand

To ensure adequate enrollment in new graduate programs, the departments we interviewed indicated they take into account student demand when proposing such programs. Departments, however, tend to engage in informal efforts to capture student demand. Few reported that they look at student enrollment in programs at other institutions similar to the one they are proposing. Departments also indicated that they survey undergraduate students regarding interest in the graduate programs they wish to propose. This type of information is subjective and unreliable as it captures, at best, student self-reported interest. Furthermore, students surveyed may know little about the range of programs available in master's and doctoral programs, the labor market demands of such programs, or opportunities for nonacademic career paths.

In instances where an institution or department and a private entity have a partnership to develop online graduate programs, the private partner tends to take a more systematic approach to estimating student demand.

It is important to consider that even if student demand is captured accurately, such a motivator is not sufficient on its own to propose a new graduate program from an economic policy perspective. An important goal of Texas's graduate programs is to meet labor market needs, not just student needs. Our case studies identified several instances where there was tension between meeting student and labor market needs. For example, one institution collected data from students that showed demand for a master's degree in general education. At the same time, education faculty have been finding that districts and schools are in need of master's degrees in specialized education content areas rather than general education. In engineering, we found the reverse: a need for master's degrees but inadequate domestic student demand. Thus, public institutions would need take into account both student and labor market demand. Defining how much attention should be given to each is critical.

Recommendations

Appropriately using student demand information to inform the expansion of programs is challenging for institutions when there is no agreed-upon measurement metric.

Identify best practices for measuring student demand. THECB could identify best practices and provide institutions guidelines on how to measure student demand.

Provide guidance on balancing student and labor market demands. THECB could also clarify for institutions how to balance the needs measured by student demand and labor market demand, especially in instances when such needs are misaligned. THECB could also help institutions identify when labor market demand should outweigh student demand and vice versa. For example, for a new research-oriented doctoral program, the labor market demand might outweigh student demand.

Emerging Multidisciplinary Fields

Our interviews suggest that there is a shift in the labor market, with some industries seeking graduates who have skills that cross the boundaries between disciplines. This shift has resulted in departments proposing multidisciplinary graduate degrees, especially in the sciences. Examples of multidisciplinary graduate degrees include GIS, data science, and specialized master's programs in engineering. These graduate degrees incorporate courses from many traditional disciplines such as statistics, computer science, engineering, geography, and urban planning, as well as others. The few employers interviewed agreed with the departments' assessment regarding the need to provide graduate students with multidisciplinary training. However, the employers questioned whether multidisciplinary training could be provided through adding a certificate; stackable, modular certificates; or elective courses to single-discipline graduate programs, instead of developing new master's degrees. A geology and hydraulics employer who hires graduates with degrees in geography and GIS emphasized this point. He indicated that those he hired with master's degrees in geography might have benefitted from having a couple of additional classes in data modeling that GIS graduates usually take as part of their program. Otherwise, their skills were similar to those of GIS graduates. Another employer was concerned that multidisciplinary programs might water down job-related fundamentals since such programs address a variety of subjects from different disciplines and might not allocate adequate time to discuss each topic in depth.

Recommendation

Certain fields need graduates with multidisciplinary skills, but whether the best way to develop those skills is through a master's degree or certification is likely to vary by field and proposed program.

Require institutions to demonstrate a need for multidisciplinary programs. When institutions propose new multidisciplinary programs, THECB could require them to conduct more rigorous analyses of labor market needs than they would normally do. This more rigorous analysis is to ensure that institutions have a good understanding of the type of multidisciplinary graduates employers are hiring and from which fields. THECB could also require institutions to articulate the benefits of the multidisciplinary program in terms of the breadth and depth of the program, the skills it promotes, and why the need being met by the proposed multidisciplinary program cannot be satisfied by restructuring existing programs in the main field through the addition of new courses or certificates, including stackable credentials.

Professional Degree Upgrading

Graduate programs in nursing and physical therapy propose new graduate degrees to respond to professional associations. These associations advocate for advanced, often doctoral, degree programs as entry to practice, usually to support and justify a greater level of professional responsibility for practitioners. Most of the nursing and physical therapy departments we interviewed agreed with association recommendations, while a few did not think such programs were needed for entry to practice. They argued that the skills taught at the master's level are adequate. However, there was agreement that professional association recommendations are likely to become requirements that employers will demand in the future. The departments that we interviewed emphasized that their responsibility is to meet employer demand and make sure their graduate students are well placed; therefore, they see a need for such programs.

Recommendation

Professional associations can be influential in shaping labor markets, especially for professional degrees in regulated occupations.

Consider professional association standards when they are likely to shape employer demand. When evaluating new graduate programs, THECB should take into account changes in professional association standards, where they exist, to the extent they are likely to shape student and employer demand.

Incentives and Barriers to Expanding Graduate Education

The structure in which institutions are embedded provides both incentives and disincentives to the expansion of graduate education. As discussed earlier, the policies and strategic plans implemented by the state, such as the *60x30TX* strategic plan, will likely signal to institutions the need to expand graduate education. The criteria THECB uses for reviewing and approving graduate programs also shapes the type of graduate programs institutions will propose. For example, given that workforce demand is one of the criteria on which proposed graduate programs are evaluated, institutions are less likely to propose graduate programs, such as those in humanities, that do not have direct links or clear paths to an occupation or multiple occupations. Whether or not the state provides increased resources for research and graduate student stipends will also affect institutions' interest in expanding graduate programs.

Furthermore, factors internal and external to the institution also play a role in facilitating and hindering graduate education expansion. Lack of adequate resources and faculty capacity can hinder institutions' efforts to expand their graduate programs. Institutions are also likely to consider the fit with their mission and student demand when deciding to expand graduate programs. Institutions that emphasize teaching might find moving into research graduate programs difficult because of misalignment with their teaching mission and a lack of institutional policies and support for research. Similarly, the extent of competition can also affect the extent to which institutions will propose new graduate programs. An institution is less likely to propose a new graduate program if other universities have similar programs and are targeting students within the same geographic areas, unless the new program has a competitive edge in terms of delivery or specialization.

6 Systemic and Process Aspects of Graduate Program Development

Our analysis examined a number of topics that go beyond the findings and recommendations related to the graduate program decisionmaking process discussed in the previous chapter. In this chapter, we examine the pipeline of students entering science and engineering graduate programs, the state funding approach for graduate programs, the proposal development process, and ongoing program review processes.

Strengthening the Pipeline of Domestic Students into Science and Engineering Graduate Programs

Our case studies show quite small numbers of domestic students enrolled in engineering graduate programs. It would be beneficial to the state to incentivize domestic students to continue their graduate education in engineering.

In contrast to foreign students who may come to the United States unaccompanied, many domestic students have family responsibilities and are concerned about meeting those responsibilities. As graduates in science, technology, engineering, and math (STEM) fields, they typically have access to good salaries after they earn their bachelor's degrees and limited incentive to pursue graduate education, at least immediately after an undergraduate program. At least one emerging research university told us it solicited foundation funding to provide extra stipends to domestic students to address their financial concerns. They were pleased with the results and hope to continue the program.

Because minority groups, especially Hispanics, are underrepresented in Texas graduate degree awards, efforts to attract more domestic students should also aim to increase the number of underrepresented students entering these graduate programs.

Recommendations

While major structural factors contribute to the low enrollment of domestic students in science and engineering graduate programs, institutions, systems, and the state could all adopt programs to strengthen this pipeline and increase the representation of domestic students in general and underrepresented minorities in particular.

Institutions and systems should consider programs to strengthen the pipeline of domestic students, including underrepresented minorities, into science and engineering graduate programs. We think institutions and systems have opportunities to collaborate to strengthen the exposure of domestic students, including underrepresented minorities, to graduate study in science and engineering. Institutions could formally collaborate by developing pipelines through articulation agreements to transition students from undergraduate to graduate degrees. More broadly, higher education and K–12 institutions should collaborate to expand the pipeline starting at the earlier stages of education.

THECB should examine plans for student stipends in new research graduate programs. Stipends are important for supporting students, especially domestic students, in research graduate programs. THECB should continue to examine proposed stipend levels to ensure that they are adequate and competitive with other quality research graduate programs. THECB should also continue to assess whether proposed programs offer credible plans for financing their proposed stipends. Evidence could include the institution's track record of financing stipends in other research graduate programs.

The state (or other funders) should consider funding special stipends for domestic students in science and engineering doctoral programs. The state, or perhaps other funders like foundations, could provide special stipends for domestic students beyond what the institutions or departments could provide. As in the example we cited above, these incentives could increase the interest of domestic students in enrolling in graduate programs. Since domestic students have options to pursue a master's degree during their career, we suggest that any special stipends be targeted specifically to domestic students in doctoral science and engineering programs (either concurrent with a master's program or following one). A portion of state research funding discussed in Chapter 4 could be devoted to funding these additional stipends to make doctoral study more attractive.

Funding

The ambitious *60x30TX* goal of increasing higher education degree and certificate awards by 80 percent over 15 years will require significant additional resources for universities and colleges. If the state does not allocate more general fund revenue, institutions will almost certainly have to increase student fees to finance the necessary expansion. Thus, it is important for the state to fund student growth to avoid such increases in cost to students.

General academic and health-related institutions receive state funding according to formulas (one for each type of institution) based on semester credit hours taught or full-time student equivalents enrolled. The formulas allocate funding according to weights for broad academic field and level of degree. The general academic formula is based on the actual cost experience of all public institutions and adjusted every two years, while the health-related formula is simplified and not adjusted over time. The different weights are intended to represent different levels of cost for teaching at higher degree levels and in more resource-intensive fields, like laboratory science.

The institutional leaders we interviewed were well aware of the operations of the formulas and realized that any formula based on statewide averages is unlikely to match the precise variations in relative costs at specific institutions. Nonetheless, there was almost no interest in changing the operation of the formulas.

Although many forms of online education may cost just as much as traditional face-to-face delivery, some highly scalable online master's programs may be able to deliver programs at a low cost per student. If such programs grow over time, they could result in significant funding under the current formula, potentially reducing the funds available to institutions that do not adopt these delivery models.

Recommendation

To meet the ambitious *60x30TX* goals of increased student enrollment and completions, institutions will require resources.

Consider increases in general fund appropriations to support growing enrollments and use the current formula funding method to allocate them. If the state provides increased general fund appropriations that keep pace with student enrollment growth, these increases will reduce the chance that students will become burdened with escalating fees. Whatever the level of general fund appropriations, we recommend that THECB continue to use the current formula funding methodology to allocate them, although it may be prudent to monitor whether highly scalable online master's programs are attracting an increasing share of formula funding over time and, if so, consider adjustments to the formula.

Proposal Development and Review Process

All the states we reviewed have an extensive development and review process for proposed new graduate programs. Although California no longer has a state-level review, Texas, Florida, and New York all require institution, system, and state approval for new graduate programs.

Our interviewees reported that the process is lengthy, often requiring a full year for the campus to develop a proposal and another year for the university system and THECB to review and act upon it. For programs that do not require full THECB review (specifically master's programs with less than $2 million in new investment), the state-level process is greatly streamlined.

Despite the length of the process, most observers thought the multiple reviews were appropriate. Several of our interviewees, however, indicated that some faculty and departments spent significant time developing proposals even in circumstances where there were major concerns about labor market demand or institutional capacity. Few of the institutions we visited have formal procedures to evaluate proposals at the initial stages, so these specific concerns might not be highlighted for many months until the proposal reaches higher levels of institution and system review. Early evaluations, or even informal feedback during proposal development, could identify specific concerns that departments should address as they develop proposals. In addition, few institutions consult informally with THECB staff prior to submitting a proposal. Such early consultations could identify a number of factors that might influence institutions' decisions to proceed with a proposal or the key questions that they need to address to gain approval. For instance, such informal consultations could help institutions learn from the experiences of other institutions in developing similar proposals and highlight specific issues that may be raised during the formal review. From our discussions with institutions and THECB staff, these issues often involve either evidence of labor market demand for a program or faculty capacity to execute it.

Institutions varied in their perceptions of the quality and usefulness of THECB staff feedback on proposals. We observed that interviewees who have personal relationships with THECB staff or whose institutional leaders (such as the provost) had well-established relationships with THECB staff seemed to report that THECB feedback was more useful. Many of these relationships seem to arise from either rotations of staff between THECB and institutions or a short fellowship program, through which institutional leaders and staff were invited to THECB to participate in proposal review for a week or so. Given the benefits of these relationships, restarting such a fellowship program may be worthwhile. Early, informal consultation on specific proposals, discussed previously, can also help to build these relationships and improve the usefulness of eventual formal THECB staff feedback.

Recommendations

The proposal process could be improved through several strategies, focusing on providing earlier, informal reviews and sharing the practices that result in successful proposals.

Institutions should conduct their own preproposal reviews. Since proposal development takes significant time, institutions should conduct internal preproposal reviews to direct proposal development efforts in the most productive directions.

Institutions should consult informally with THECB staff early during proposal development. Similarly, institutions should seek early, informal consultation with THECB staff to understand the experiences of other similar proposal efforts and receive guidance on which aspects of a proposal are likely to receive the greatest scrutiny. These informal consultations should not extend the time required for proposal review, and ideally, they will reduce it.

Provide guidance on the characteristics of successful proposals. To generalize and extend the consultation function, THECB could compile guidance on the aspects associated with the most successful proposals. This guidance could help institutions and departments as they prepare future proposals.

Ongoing Program Review Processes

THECB generally has limited powers to review programs after they have been approved, with two major exceptions: periodic doctoral program reviews and low-producing programs. Doctoral programs are required to report to THECB annually for five years and then at least every seven years after that point.

Under the recent revisions to its mandate, THECB no longer has the authority to order the closure of degree programs with low enrollment or production. Instead, the state now relies on an annual THECB report on low-producing programs that identifies degree programs at each institution that have been operating at least five years and whose number of graduates has fallen below a specified threshold over a five-year period (25 for undergraduate, 15 for master's, and 10 for doctoral). If a particular program appears on this report for three consecutive years, THECB staff may issue a recommendation to close the program or consolidate it with other related programs to increase enrollment and graduation. If the institution does not accept the THECB staff recommendation, it must report to the legislature on its decision and provide either an action plan to increase the number of graduates or a rationale for maintaining the small program.

Institutional leadership told us that they pay close attention to this low-producing program report. Many of them said they try to anticipate which small programs may appear on the report before it is produced. They develop strategies to strengthen, consolidate, or close such programs to avoid having them appear on the report or, if they do appear, to avoid having them appear for three consecutive years, which would require formal action.

While consolidating small programs can reduce administrative and academic overhead and fixed costs and can develop a critical mass of graduate students with a common experience, a number of institutions told us that some of their consolidations were largely cosmetic exercises to combine loosely related small programs to avoid appearing on the low-producing programs report. Such consolidations probably provide little benefit in reducing overhead and fixed costs. And since they generally require all students to earn the same degree title, albeit with opportunities to designate a specialization, some of these consolidations can make marketing themselves to employers harder for students.

A few departments also told us that they addressed low-producing programs by lowering admission standards to expand enrollment.

Recommendation

Continue policies and practices for program review and low-producing programs; review consolidation proposals closely. The doctoral program review and low-producing programs report seem to be helpful in managing graduate programs. One area we recommend for further scrutiny is proposed consolidations of graduate programs to ensure that they entail meaningful integration of the academic programs.

Syda Productions/Fotolia

7 Conclusion

Texas has a large and complex higher education ecosystem. Unlike some other states that benefit from prestigious private universities, Texas depends very heavily on its public universities to train graduates, produce research, and spur innovation in the state economy. As a result, policies affecting the public university sector are especially important in maintaining and enhancing Texas's state competitiveness.

Graduate education has been growing strongly in Texas over the past ten years, and Texas's *60x30TX* strategic plan and our analysis of labor market projections point to continued strong growth of graduate education in the state. The top occupational groups are expected to be business, healthcare, education, computers, and engineering. Generally, Texas has been increasing its production of graduate degrees in corresponding fields, although growth in graduate engineering degrees has been slow compared to other states and to projected demand. THECB and institutions might want to consider expanding graduate programs in engineering, especially to recruit domestic students. Such programs would need to provide adequate financial support to motivate domestic students with a bachelor's degree to pursue graduate education.

Texas's position compared to other states and countries is important to its state competitiveness. While Texas is increasing its number of research universities quickly compared to other states, it is still not represented at the highest levels of international competition and does not attract the same share of federal R&D funding, especially compared to California. If Texas desires to further increase the competitiveness of its universities, it will likely need additional public investments in research capacity. The state should support institutions at several stages of development, but to be productive, these investments must be focused on institutions with at least some level of demonstrated capability in developing research programs.

Some of Texas's needed expansion can come from expanding enrollments in existing programs, but some will likely come from new programs. Developing new programs presents the state and institutions with both opportunities and challenges. Expanding graduate programs and research is an opportunity to serve state economic needs and build institutional prestige, but it can also lead to unproductive prestige-seeking behavior, with institutions focusing on graduate education and research not for their contributions to the state and nation but to advance in rankings for their own sake. Pressure to increase operating margins in the face of constrained state funding can also lead to the development of large-scale online programs. While these programs may expand access, they may also dilute quality to earn revenues. For all these reasons, it is important to evaluate proposals for new graduate programs to ensure that they maximize the benefits to Texas and the United States.

Orienting a university toward a research-intensive mission requires a widespread and sustained institutional commitment. So asking institutions embarking on this path to develop a thoughtful strategic plan and align their graduate program proposals with that plan is appropriate. Other universities may productively focus on specific niches where they can offer graduate degree programs that cater to their specific capabilities or context and that may not be available widely.

As Texas graduate education grows and especially as online delivery becomes more common, managing competition and promoting quality in graduate programs is important for institutions and systems. In terms of proposal development, institutions would benefit from earlier, informal review of their proposals both internally and with THECB. Such reviews could highlight the need to improve analysis of labor market demand and institutional capacity for graduate programs. Finally, in science and engineering fields where international students represent the majority, the state and its higher education systems should consider ways to strengthen the pipeline of domestic students, perhaps with financial incentives to encourage them to undertake graduate study.

goodluz/Fotolia

APPENDIX

A Detailed Tables

Table A.1. *Study Data Sources*

Data Source	Details
Quantitative	
Texas Higher Education Coordinating Board (THECB)	THECB provided information on degree completions and program proposals.
Higher Education Research and Development Survey	The National Science Foundation's National Center for Science and Engineering Statistics collects data on R&D expenditures by state, institutional control, and institution. We analyzed data from fiscal years 2004–13.
Academic Ranking of World Universities	ShanghaiRanking Consultancy uses objective indicators of universities' research excellence and alumni success to rank the top 500 universities in the world. We analyzed data from 2005 and 2014.
Carnegie Classification of Institutions of Higher Education	Indiana University Center for Postsecondary Research now manages the Carnegie Classification system to categorize higher education institutions in the United States. We analyzed data from 2005 and 2015.
Integrated Postsecondary Education System (IPEDS)	The National Center for Education Statistics IPEDS provides detailed graduate degree completion data and institutional characteristics for higher education institutions. We analyzed data from 2005 and 2014.
American Community Survey (ACS)	The ACS, published by the U.S. Census Bureau, provides data on the share of workers with a graduate degree by occupation at the national, state, and local levels. We used Texas data from 2005 to 2012 to obtain graduate shares.
Occupational Employment Projections, U.S. Bureau of Labor Statistics	The Bureau of Labor Statistics publishes ten-year occupational employment projections. We analyzed data for 2012–22.
Occupational Employment Projections, Texas Workforce Commission	The Texas Workforce Commission publishes ten-year occupational employment projections. We analyzed data for 2012–22.
Occupational Employment Projections, Florida Department of Economic Opportunity	Florida's Department of Economic Opportunity publishes long-term occupational employment projections. We analyzed data for 2015–23.
Occupational Employment Projections, New York Department of Labor	New York's Department of Labor publishes ten-year occupational employment projections. We analyzed data for 2012–22.
Occupational Employment Projections, State of California Employment Development Department	California's Employment Development Department publishes ten-year occupational employment projections. We analyzed data for 2012–22.
Qualitative	
Stakeholder interviews	Interviewees included presidents/vice presidents, provosts/associate provosts, deans of graduate schools, department chairs/associate chairs, college deans/associate deans, program directors/associate directors, Texas university system leaders, university system leaders in California and New York, and employers.
University of Texas (UT) system administration	The UT administration provides information on policies governing new program proposal development and approval.
Texas A&M system administration	The A&M administration provides information on policies governing new program proposal development and approval.

Data Source	Details
Florida Department of Higher Education	The Florida Department of Higher Education provides information on Florida's higher education system organization, administration, legislation, and oversight. It also provides information on the approval process and related policies associated with new graduate programs.
Florida State University (FSU) system administration	The FSU administration provides an overview of policies governing new program proposal development and approval.
Florida College System (FCS) administration	The FCS administration provides an overview of policies governing new program proposal development and approval.
Office of College and University Evaluation, New York State Department of Education	The Office of College and University Evaluation provides information on New York's higher education system organization, administration, legislation, and oversight. It also provides information on the approval process and related policies associated with new graduate programs.
State University of New York (SUNY) system administration	The SUNY administration provides an overview of policies governing new program proposal development and approval.
City University of New York (CUNY) system administration	The CUNY administration provides an overview of policies governing new program proposal development and approval.
State of California, Legislative Analyst's Office (LAO)	The LAO provides the legislation and implementation details surrounding California's Master Plan for Higher Education, which governs the structure of higher education offerings and institutional hierarchy in California.
University of California (UC) system administration	The UC administration provides an overview of policies governing new program proposal development and approval.
California State University (CSU) system administration	The CSU administration provides an overview of policies governing new program proposal development and approval.

Table A.2. *Projected Graduate Demand in Texas, 2012–22*

SOC	Occupation	Group	Employment, 2012	Growth, 2006–13 (percentage)	Graduate Share, 2012 (percentage)	Projected Employment Change, 2012–22	Projected New Graduate Employment, 2012–22
23-1011	Lawyers	Lawyers	49,350	N/A	100.0	10,740	10,740
25-2021	Elementary School Teachers, Ex. Special Education	Teachers	141,030	21	25.4	39,890	10,100
11-1000	Top Executives	Business	183,810	7	24.3	40,260	9,800
31-1000	Nursing, Psychiatric, & Home Health Aides	Healthcare	157,590	N/A	19.8	48,190	9,500
13-2011	Accountants & Auditors	Business	105,840	15	23.2	25,410	5,900
25-2031	Secondary School Teachers, Ex. Special/Career/Technical Ed	Teachers	98,600	6	27.6	20,210	5,600
25-1071	Health Specialties Teachers, Postsecondary	Postsecondary Faculty	18,610	27	69.0	7,630	5,300
25-2022	Middle School Teachers, Ex. Special/Career/Technical Ed	Teachers	70,370	21	25.4	19,960	5,100
29-1069	Physicians & Surgeons, All Other	Healthcare	18,510	20	97.7	5,110	5,000
11-1021	General & Operations Managers	Business	172,320	N/A	12.2	38,400	4,700
29-1141	Registered Nurses	Healthcare	189,380	N/A	8.7	53,480	4,700
15-1121	Computer Systems Analysts	Computer	44,140	N/A	21.9	13,960	3,100
21-2011	Clergy	Miscellaneous	32,770	9	38.7	7,320	2,800
21-1012	Educational, Guidance, School, & Vocational Counselors	Teachers	22,030	17	57.5	4,850	2,800
13-1111	Management Analysts	Business	37,350	46	29.6	9,360	2,800
11-9032	Education Administrators, Elementary/Secondary School	Teachers	22,430	N/A	56.2	4,600	2,600
29-1127	Speech-Language Pathologists	Healthcare	11,930	101	73.7	3,060	2,300
29-1051	Pharmacists	Healthcare	19,950	23	46.5	4,700	2,200
29-1171	Nurse Practitioners	Healthcare	6,590	N/A	79.0	2,670	2,100
13-1161	Market Research Analysts & Marketing Specialists	Business	24,010	N/A	21.3	9,840	2,100
17-2171	Petroleum Engineers	Engineers	19,280	N/A	22.0	8,730	1,900
13-1199	Business Operations Specialists, All Other	Business	65,010	N/A	14.8	12,940	1,900
17-2051	Civil Engineers	Engineers	23,410	25	26.7	7,130	1,900
29-1123	Physical Therapists	Healthcare	11,660	48	50.5	3,750	1,900
13-2051	Financial Analysts	Business	20,130	60	42.0	4,430	1,900
25-1191	Graduate Teaching Assistants	Miscellaneous	17,640	27	69.0	2,620	1,800

SOC	Occupation	Group	Employment, 2012	Growth, 2006–13 (percentage)	Graduate Share, 2012 (percentage)	Projected Employment Change, 2012–22	Projected New Graduate Employment, 2012–22
15-1132	Software Developers, Applications	Computer	40,580	N/A	17.1	10,200	1,700
19-2042	Geoscientists, Ex. Hydrologists & Geographers	Engineers	10,250	14	54.2	3,090	1,700
25-3098	Substitute Teachers	Teachers	49,740	33	15.5	10,090	1,600
25-1194	Vocational Education Teachers, Postsecondary	Postsecondary Faculty	12,300	27	69.0	2,190	1,500
15-1133	Software Developers, Systems Software	Computer	32,240	N/A	17.1	8,240	1,400
11-9111	Medical & Health Services Managers	Business	19,120	42	24.2	5,780	1,400
29-1062	Family & General Practitioners	Healthcare	6,370	20	97.7	1,280	1,300
11-9041	Architectural & Engineering Managers	Business	15,450	20	32.4	3,700	1,200
29-1021	Dentists, General	Healthcare	8,970	35	98.7	1,190	1,200
25-1072	Nursing Instructors & Teachers, Postsecondary	Postsecondary Faculty	4,060	27	69.0	1,690	1,200
19-3031	Clinical, Counseling, & School Psychologists	Healthcare	7,560	-2	91.9	1,250	1,100
13-2052	Personal Financial Advisors	Business	15,320	22	25.5	4,490	1,100
29-1071	Physician Assistants	Healthcare	5,470	14	46.3	2,410	1,100
25-4021	Librarians	Teachers	10,240	-1	55.9	1,990	1,100
11-3031	Financial Managers	Business	29,610	N/A	17.3	6,420	1,100
11-3021	Computer & Information Systems Managers	Business	17,840	N/A	22.7	4,260	1,000

SOURCE: RAND calculations from TWC and ACS data.

Note: N/A indicates not available in the ACS data.

Table A.3. *Graduate Degree Completions by State and Broad Field, 2005 and 2014*

	2005				2014			
Broad Field	TX	CA	FL	NY	TX	CA	FL	NY
Business	9,049	11,816	7,472	10,186	13,411	17,720	11,001	14,348
Education	7,611	14,215	7,074	20,433	9,923	14,508	5,558	16,673
Engineering	3,421	5,922	2,544	2,758	4,139	8,263	4,123	4,600
Fine Arts	761	2,098	468	2,966	968	3,305	1,054	3,773
Health	5,214	7,530	4,279	8,303	9,102	13,566	7,962	13,730
Legal	2,652	5,483	2,395	5,785	2,485	6,011	3,285	5,845
Liberal Arts	4,001	6,811	1,518	6,798	5,113	8,803	2,530	8,320
Science	3,413	6,418	1,764	5,187	5,676	7,986	2,856	7,035
Social Science	4,515	8,890	3,213	10,374	6,859	14,747	4,838	12,303
Total	**40,149**	**66,423**	**28,466**	**72,434**	**56,592**	**83,408**	**39,577**	**85,519**

SOURCE: RAND calculations from IPEDS data.

Table A.4. *Growth Rates of Graduate Degree Completions by State and Broad Field, 2005–14*

	Growth Rate (2005–14)			
Broad Field	TX	CA	FL	NY
Business	45%	24%	53%	37%
Education	30%	-10%	-18%	-18%
Engineering	21%	40%	62%	67%
Fine Arts	27%	21%	25%	19%
Health	76%	59%	81%	67%
Legal	-6%	9%	25%	1%
Liberal Arts	28%	24%	49%	22%
Science	66%	23%	64%	35%
Social Science	51%	61%	50%	18%
Total	**41%**	**26%**	**39%**	**18%**

SOURCE: RAND calculations from IPEDS data.

APPENDIX

B Findings on Six Case Study Fields

Nursing

Degrees Awarded

In nursing, Texas public institutions awarded a total of 1,710 graduate degrees in academic year 2013–14. Of these, 1,542 were master's degrees, and the remaining 168 were doctorates (including research doctorates and professional doctorates). Degrees in nursing practice were by far the most common, although a number of degrees were awarded in nursing administration and education. Table B.1 provides details of the degrees awarded.

Table B.1. *Graduate Degree Completions in Nursing Fields, Texas Public Institutions, Academic Year 2013–14*

Academic Field	Degrees Awarded		
	Master's	Doctoral	Total
Family Practice Nurse/Nursing	1,036		1,036
Nursing Administration	312		312
Nursing Education	153		153
Nursing Practice		81	81
Nursing Science		71	71
Nurse Anesthetist	17	16	33
Clinical Nurse Leader	12		12
Registered Nursing/Registered Nurse	8		8
Clinical Nurse Specialist	2		2
Nurse Midwife/Nursing Midwifery	2		2
Total	**1,542**	**168**	**1,710**

SOURCE: RAND calculations from THECB completions data.

Employment in Related Occupations and Projected Growth

Projected growth in nursing varies between 28 percent and 41 percent depending on the occupation. It is expected that there will be a need for a total of 21,100 registered nurses with graduate degrees by 2022.[8] Table B.2 provides other detailed information regarding employment needs.

8 Estimated by (graduate share of graduate nurses in 2012 * projected employment of registered nurses in 2022)/100.

Table B.2. *Employment Projections in Nursing, 2012–22*

SOC	Occupation	Employment, 2012	Graduate Share, 2012 (percentage)	Projected Employment, 2022	Projected Change, 2012–22	Projected Growth, 2012–22 (percentage)
29-1141	Registered Nurses	189,380	8.7	242,860	53,480	28.2
29-1151	Nurse Anesthetists	3,100	79.0	4,110	1,010	32.6
29-1161	Nurse Midwives	200	86.6	270	70	35.0
29-1171	Nurse Practitioners	6,590	86.6	9,260	2,670	40.5
11-9111	Medical and Health Services Managers	19,120	24.2	24,900	5,780	30.2

SOURCE: TWC and ACS data. Some graduate shares are computed from combined occupations.

Employment Setting

One of Texas' strongest economic sectors is healthcare. According to the interviews, opportunities for healthcare professionals—nurses in particular—are plentiful throughout the state. However, study interviews indicate there are shortages in the number of nurses in Texas to meet the labor market demand, especially in rural areas and pockets of metropolitan areas that have underserved populations (e.g., areas with aging populations). According to the interviews, providing adequate salaries and incentives to recruit nurses into these areas is difficult.

Nurses with master's degrees, including nurse practitioners and nurse administrators, can find jobs in many different settings such as hospitals, doctors' offices, home care, schools, and insurance providers and can serve as consultants for case management and risk. Nurses with a nurse educator certificate can find jobs as instructors at community colleges. However, the case study interviews indicate that academic settings pay a very small portion of what nurses can earn in the field, which contributes to the shortage of nurse educators. Nurses with professional doctorates have positions in health organizations where they translate research into protocols. They have leadership positions and have more opportunities for advancement. Nurses with Ph.D. degrees have job opportunities in clinical research or academia at four-year colleges, although they are limited compared to other nursing graduate degrees.

Perception of Quality and Need for Graduate Programs in Nursing

All those interviewed indicated the need for nursing graduate programs to respond to professional association requirements that advocate for advanced degrees (e.g., professional doctoral degree programs) as entry to practice. These requirements are likely to affect employer demand in future, and thus there is a need to increase the nursing student pool in the graduate programs. However, colleges are forced to turn aspiring nurses away, even if they are qualified, because of lack of institutional resource capacity, opportunities for clinical placements, and adequate numbers of faculty or nurse educators to teach graduate courses. Those interviewed also indicated the need to develop graduate programs that transition nursing students with bachelor's degrees to doctoral degrees. These programs would accelerate the time for obtaining doctoral degrees to respond to the professional associations' calls for advanced nursing graduate degrees.

Although not all nursing programs included in the study systematically seek input from employers to inform the nursing programs, standards are in place to ensure quality. Doctoral graduate programs are accredited by the Commission on Collegiate Nursing Education while the master's programs incorporate standards from the national board to ensure student success in passing the exams.

There has been an increase in online master's and professional doctorate nursing programs to improve student access as well as increase institutions' competitive edge. Study institutions varied in how the online programs were structured. Some required students to attend campus for two to three days per semester, while others were virtual programs. Institutions interviewed also indicated that credit hours for the same online programs varied considerably across institutions.

Physical Therapy

Degrees Awarded

In physical therapy, Texas public institutions awarded a total of 473 graduate degrees in academic year 2013–14. Of these, 9 were research doctorates, and the remaining 464 were professional doctorates.

Employment in Related Occupations and Projected Growth

In physical therapy, employment is projected to grow 32 percent. It is expected that there will be a need for 3,750 new physical therapists by 2022.[9] Because of licensing requirements, all of them will require a graduate degree.

Table B.3. *Employment Projections in Physical Therapy, 2012–22*

SOC	Occupation	Employment, 2012	Graduate Share, 2012 (percentage)	Projected Employment, 2022	Projected Change, 2012–22	Projected Growth, 2012–22 (percentage)
29-1123	Physical Therapists	11,660	50.5	15,410	3,750	32.2

SOURCE: TWC and ACS data.

Employment Setting

Opportunities for careers in physical therapy are available throughout the state. The need for physical therapists is heightened by greater demand for healthcare in general among an aging population. Physical therapists work in a variety of settings including hospitals, rehabilitation facilities, sports training facilities, outpatient clinics, schools, homes, and hospices. Whether they have a master's degree or a professional doctoral degree, physical therapists work within the same settings.

Perception of Quality and Need for Graduate Programs in Physical Therapy

As with nursing, the physical therapy departments in the study indicated the need for professional doctorate programs to respond to professional association requirements for advanced degrees as entry to practice to promote professionalism for the occupation. These requirements are likely to affect employer demand in future, and thus there is a need to increase the number of students in the professional doctorate programs. However, some programs reported that they are facing challenges in expanding their student pool due to an insufficient number of faculty. There is less need for Ph.D. degrees in physical therapy.

9 Estimated by (graduate share in 2012 * projected employment in 2022)/100.

In regards to quality, the physical therapy programs examined in the study are accredited by the Commission on Accreditation for Physical Therapy Education. The employer interviewed indicated that the graduate programs across the public institutions in Texas promote students' analytic and problem-solving skills, which are critical to the occupation. However, according to the employer there is a need for the programs to focus on developing the social skills and hands-on experience of students in the graduate programs. Universities struggle to get students into clinics. As a result, graduates lack rigorous exposure to complex care. To compensate, the employer provides training in acute care during their first year of employment.

Education

Degrees Awarded

In K–12 education and school leadership fields (the specific fields we selected for this study), Texas public institutions awarded a total of 5,862 graduate degrees in academic year 2013–14. Of these, 5,334 were master's degrees, and the remaining 528 were doctorates (including research doctorates and professional doctorates). Table B.4 provides details of the degrees awarded.

Table B.4. *Graduate Degree Completions in K–12 Education Fields, Texas Public Institutions, Academic Year 2013–14*

Academic Field	Degrees Awarded		
	Master's	Doctoral	Total
Educational Leadership and Administration, General	2,265	289	2,554
Curriculum and Instruction	1,152	115	1,267
Special Education and Teaching, General	524	34	558
Educational/Instructional Technology	356	6	362
Elementary Education and Teaching	184	19	203
Secondary Education and Teaching	168		168
Early Childhood Education and Teaching	145	6	151
Physical Education Teaching and Coaching	92		92
Teaching English as a Second or Foreign Language	84		84
Bilingual and Multilingual Education	66	2	68
Other	298	57	355
Total	**5,334**	**528**	**5,862**

SOURCE: RAND calculations from THECB completions data.

Employment in Related Occupations and Projected Growth

Projected growth in education varies between 19 percent and 28 percent depending on the occupation. It is expected that there will be a need for a total of 117,600[10] teachers and 17,000[11] administrators with graduate degrees by 2022. Table B.5 provides other detailed information regarding employment needs.

10 For each teacher category, graduate share in 2012 was multiplied by projected employment in 2022 and divided by 100. We then summed the projected need of graduates across all teacher categories.

11 For each administrator category, graduate share in 2012 was multiplied by projected employment in 2022 and divided by 100. We then summed the projected need of graduates across all administrator categories.

Table B.5. *Employment Projections in Education, 2012–22*

SOC	Occupation	Employment, 2012	Graduate Share, 2012 (percentage)	Projected Employment, 2022	Projected Change, 2012–22	Projected Growth, 2012–22 (percentage)
25-2011	Preschool Teachers, Ex. Special Education	20,390	5.8	24,970	4,580	22.5
25-2012	Kindergarten Teachers, Ex. Special Education	13,790	5.8	17,680	3,890	28.2
25-2021	Elementary School Teachers, Ex. Special Education	141,030	25.4	180,920	39,890	28.3
25-2022	Middle School Teachers, Ex. Special/Career/Technical Ed	70,370	25.4	90,330	19,960	28.4
25-2023	Career/Technical Education Teachers, Middle School	1,470	25.4	1,770	300	20.4
25-2031	Secondary School Teachers, Ex. Special/Career/Technical Ed	98,600	27.6	118,810	20,210	20.5
25-2032	Career/Technical Education Teachers, Secondary School	9,860	27.6	11,840	1,980	20.1
25-2051	Special Education Teachers, Preschool	1,000	30.3	1,220	220	22.0
25-2052	Special Education Teachers, Kindergarten & Elementary School	11,970	30.3	14,380	2,410	20.1
25-2053	Special Education Teachers, Middle School	5,500	30.3	6,610	1,110	20.2
25-2054	Special Education Teachers, Secondary School	8,240	30.3	9,830	1,590	19.3
11-9031	Education Administrators, Preschool/Childcare Center/Program	2,620	56.2	3,170	550	21.0
11-9032	Education Administrators, Elementary/Secondary School	22,430	56.2	27,030	4,600	20.5

SOURCE: TWC and ACS data. Some graduate shares are computed from combined occupations.

Employment Setting

According to the interviews, teaching jobs have been increasing in Texas even with the economic downturn. However, the education sector is experiencing shortages of teachers and principals due to increases in student population and educator retirements. Shortages are prominent in rural areas, where salaries are not comparable to those in metropolitan areas. There is less demand for superintendents due to the limited number of such positions and superintendents' average job span.

Texas, unlike many other states, does not require a master's degree for teachers at entry or later career stages. According to the employers and higher education administrators we interviewed, salaries are similar for teachers with bachelor's and master's degrees. Master's degrees might open up opportunities for teachers to take more instructional leadership responsibilities (e.g., teacher mentor or instructional coach) at their schools. Educators with a professional doctorate in education (Ed.D.) are usually hired as school or district leaders or community college leaders (e.g., principals, instructional leaders at the district level). Those who have Ph.D. degrees are hired in academia, although faculty opportunities are limited.

Perception of Quality and Need for Graduate Programs in Education

According to education department and employer interviews, the quality of education graduate programs varies by institution. Institutions raised concerns about the quality of some of the online graduate programs established by private–public partnerships in terms of large class sizes, lack of qualifications of instructors teaching the courses, and the fact that those online programs are accelerated. Institutions were also concerned about the increase in alternative certifications by regional centers. They viewed such programs as lacking the rigor to train prospective teachers on how be effective in the classroom.

Regarding the need for graduate programs in education, one employer indicated that he sees better teaching and student learning outcomes for teachers with master's degrees than for those who have only a bachelor's degree. The employer also indicated that school districts are currently seeking teachers with specialized advanced degrees in subjects such as math or reading and not broader education graduate degrees. He advocated for schools of education to emphasize subject specialties in their graduate degrees or partner with subject matter programs (e.g., math or English) for joint graduate programs.

Electrical Engineering

Degrees Awarded

In electrical and electronics engineering, Texas public institutions awarded a total of 938 graduate degrees in academic year 2013–14. Of these, 725 were master's degrees, and the remaining 213 were doctorates.

Employment in Related Occupations and Projected Growth

Projected growth in electrical engineering/electronic engineering is about 23 percent. It is expected that there will be a need for at least 8,400 electrical engineers with graduate degrees by 2022.[12] Table B.6 provides detailed information regarding employment needs.

Table B.6. *Employment Projections in Electrical Engineering, 2012–22*

SOC	Occupation	Employment, 2012	Graduate Share, 2012 (percentage)	Projected Employment, 2022	Projected Change, 2012–22	Projected Growth, 2012–22 (percentage)
17-2071	Electrical Engineers	13,620	27.7	16,450	2,830	20.8
17-2072	Electronics Engineers, Ex. Computer	11,110	27.7	13,580	2,470	22.2
11-9041	Architectural and Engineering Managers	15,450	32.4	19,150	3,700	23.9

SOURCE: TWC and ACS data. Some graduate shares are computed from combined occupations.

Employment Setting

Because of Texas's role in energy production, there is a need for engineers in the energy sector and other sectors that grow as a result of the energy sector (e.g., technology and manufacturing). Among the engineering fields, the largest workforce needs are petroleum engineers, electrical/electronics and computer engineers, mechanical engineers, civil engineers, and industrial engineers. Study institutions offer graduate programs in the engineering fields mentioned. Because the engineering job market is strong, graduates with bachelor's and master's degrees sometimes compete for the same jobs and salaries. According to faculty and employers, the advantage of the master's degrees is that graduates can work more effectively in lab settings because of their research training. Further, a master's degree provides opportunities for graduates to lead

12 For electrical engineers and electronics engineers, each graduate share in 2012 was multiplied by projected employment in 2022 and divided by 100. We then summed the projected need of graduates across both categories.

teams and get promoted at their jobs. There are limited positions in the industry for graduates with Ph.D. degrees. Usually doctoral graduates seek faculty positions.

The engineering departments in the study indicated that they work closely with the businesses in the industry to ensure that graduates have jobs. Usually master's students intern at these businesses to develop needed occupational soft and technical skills. This experience provides an opportunity for them to get hired at the businesses where they interned.

Perception of Quality and Need for Graduate Programs in Electrical Engineering

The department and employer interviews emphasized the need for graduate programs in electrical engineering, especially since domestic students with bachelor's degrees in engineering tend not to pursue postgraduate work. Graduate engineering programs tend to enroll a much larger proportion of international students than domestic students, unlike undergraduate engineering programs. This shift in enrollment is because engineering departments do not have the funding available to provide support to domestic students that is comparable to the salaries that are available for engineers with bachelor's degrees. International students, on the other hand, are satisfied with the support provided as they may have fewer financial needs or make sacrifices to come to the United States.

The study engineering departments indicated that they have advisory boards representing the industry informing their curriculum. Having an advisory board ensures that the curriculum is relevant to the industry. One employer highlighted a few areas where graduate engineering programs could improve: (1) Structure the programs so they balance theory with application, (2) hire faculty from the industry, (3) have faculty and students engage in more project-based and hands-on activities, and (4) infuse business courses into the program so that graduates have an understanding of the finance and business aspects of engineering tasks and products.

Unlike the healthcare graduate programs and education, online graduate programs are not common in engineering as there is a concern about how to offer labs and implement application activities virtually.

Statistics

Degrees Awarded

In statistics fields, Texas public institutions awarded a total of 159 graduate degrees in academic year 2013–14. Of these, 133 were master's degrees, and the remaining 26 were doctorates. Table B.7 provides details of the degrees awarded.

Table B.7. *Graduate Degree Completions in Statistics Fields, Texas Public Institutions, Academic Year 2013–14*

Academic Field	Degrees Awarded		
	Master's	Doctoral	Total
Statistics, General	101	19	120
Biostatistics	32	7	39
Total	**133**	**26**	**159**

SOURCE: RAND calculations from THECB completions data.

Employment in Related Occupations and Projected Growth

Projected growth in statistics is about 37 percent. It is expected that there will be a need for at least 550 statisticians with graduate degrees by 2022.[13] In addition, statistics graduates may be employed in many other occupations.

Table B.8. *Employment Projections in Statistics, 2012–22*

SOC	Occupation	Employment, 2012	Graduate Share, 2012 (percentage)	Projected Employment, 2022	Projected Change, 2012–22	Projected Growth, 2012–22 (percentage)
15-2041	Statisticians	850	47.5	1,160	310	36.5

SOURCE: TWC and ACS data.

Employment Setting

According to our interviews, the field of statistics is increasingly critical to academia, businesses, and governments to accommodate the escalating dependence on data-driven decisions. An attractive aspect of the statistics profession is that it can apply to a variety of career pathways. For example, statisticians could be hired by universities, government agencies, research centers, statistical software developers, banks, insurance companies, hospitals, or pharmaceutical companies. The study interviews suggest that there might be competition between statisticians and social scientists trained in statistics. According to an employer, statisticians and social scientists trained in statistics are increasingly doing the same work.

Perception of Quality and Need for Graduate Programs in Statistics

According to statistics department and employer interviews, there is need for statisticians at both the master's and doctoral levels because of the job opportunities available. Jobs that require the application of statistical approaches seek graduates with master's degrees, while jobs that require the application of a deeper theoretical understanding and the creation of new and innovative procedures seek Ph.D. graduates.

The employer interviewed indicated that the statistics graduate programs in Texas public universities vary in quality, but some are very strong. Overall, the programmatic areas that need improvement are related not to the subject matter but to improving graduate statisticians' writing abilities.

13 Estimated by (graduate share in 2012 * projected employment in 2022)/100.

Geographic Information Science (GIS)

Degrees Awarded

In geography and GIS, Texas public institutions awarded a total of 89 graduate degrees in academic year 2013–14. Of these, 63 were master's degrees, and the remaining 26 were doctorates. Table B.9 provides details of the degrees awarded.

Table B.9. *Graduate Degree Completions in GIS Fields, Texas Public Institutions, Academic Year 2013–14*

	Degrees Awarded		
Academic Field	Master's	Doctoral	Total
Geography	36	22	58
Geographic Information Science and Cartography	27	4	31
Total	**63**	**26**	**89**

SOURCE: RAND calculations from THECB completions data.

Employment in Related Occupations and Projected Growth

Projected growth in GIS-related occupations varies between 18 percent and 46 percent, depending on the occupation. This is an emerging field so the occupations do not necessarily reflect demand specifically for GIS. Table B.10 provides detailed information regarding employment needs for some potentially related occupations.

Table B.10. *Employment Projections in GIS, 2012–22*

SOC	Occupation	Employment, 2012	Graduate Share, 2012 (percentage)	Projected Employment, 2022	Projected Change, 2012–22	Projected Growth, 2012–22 (percentage)
19-2042	Geoscientists, Ex. Hydrologists & Geographers	10,250	54.2	13,340	3,090	30.1
19-3092	Geographers	130	38.4	190	60	46.2
11-9121	Natural Sciences Managers	1,680	72.8	1,980	300	17.9

SOURCE: TWC and ACS data.

Employment Setting

According to interviews with GIS department leaders and employers, the GIS sector, although currently small, is expected to grow in Texas. Currently, the oil and gas industry is responsible for a large number of geospatial jobs in Texas. For example, energy/petroleum corporations in the Houston area (e.g., Shell, Mobile, and Chevron) hire individuals with GIS experience. The areas of Austin, Houston, and Dallas also are home to a large number of consulting firms that provide geospatial support to the petroleum industry. As with other urban areas, these cities also support a number of academic, local government, and private-sector GIS jobs.

Perception of Quality and Need for Graduate Programs in GIS

Because GIS is a multidisciplinary field, GIS graduate programs could be housed in a variety of departments or colleges including civil engineering, science, geography, or urban planning. Departments we interviewed vary in how they structure their GIS programs. Some departments provide GIS master's degrees; others provide a master's degree in the main field such as geography and offer a separate GIS certificate for those who want to specialize in the area. Less common is having GIS programs that offer Ph.D. degrees. GIS programs are offered either face-to-face or online, depending on the department.

One of the employers interviewed indicated that he viewed GIS programs in Texas to be of good quality. Although the employer indicated the need for prospective candidates with GIS specialization as the workforce needs increase, many of the GIS positions at the company do not require graduate degrees (but a master's degree could be considered an advantage). A bachelor's degree in a GIS or related field is sufficient as long as graduates have been trained in programming. The employer also indicated that when hiring for GIS positions the company does not favor those with GIS degrees over those who have degrees in the main related fields. The employer looks at the overall attributes of the job candidate. Thus, there might not be a need for a large number of separate GIS graduate programs. Restructuring related main fields, such as by adding a couple of courses that teach students how to use GIS tools, might be adequate.

References

Brewer, Dominic J., Susan M. Gates, and Charles A. Goldman, *In Pursuit of Prestige: Strategy and Competition in U.S. Higher Education,* New Brunswick, NJ: Transaction Press, 2002.

Carnevale, Anthony P., Jeff Strohl, and Michelle Melton, *What's It Worth? The Economic Value of College Majors, 2011.* As of September 5, 2016: https://cew.georgetown.edu/wp-content/uploads/2014/11/whatsitworth-complete.pdf

Council of Graduate Schools and Educational Testing Service, *Pathways Through Graduate School and Into Careers: Report from the Commission on Pathways Through Graduate School and Into Careers,* Princeton, N.J.: Educational Testing Service, 2012.

Goldman, Charles A., Lindsay Butterfield, Diana Lavery, Trey Miller, Lindsay Daugherty, Trinidad Beleche, and Bing Han, *Using Workforce Information for Degree Program Planning in Texas,* Santa Monica, Calif.: RAND Corporation, RR-1011-CFAT, 2015. As of August 30, 2016: http://www.rand.org/pubs/research_reports/RR1011.html

McEntee, Kyle, "Law Grads Still Face a Tough Job Market," *Bloomberg Law,* May 4, 2016. As of September 5, 2016: https://bol.bna.com/law-grads-still-face-a-tough-job-market/

Olson, Elizabeth, "Burdened With Debt, Law School Graduates Struggle in Job Market," *New York Times,* April 26, 2015. As of September 5, 2016: http://www.nytimes.com/2015/04/27/business/dealbook/burdened-with-debt-law-school-graduates-struggle-in-job-market.html

Salmi, Jamil, *The Challenge of Establishing World-Class Universities,* Washington, D.C.: The World Bank, 2009.

Texas Higher Education Coordinating Board, *60x30TX, Texas Higher Education Strategic Plan: 2015–2030,* Texas Higher Education Coordinating Board, 2015a.

Texas Higher Education Coordinating Board, *Research Funding in Texas: Overview,* Texas Higher Education Coordinating Board, 2015b.